Hunting the Whole Way Home

SYDNEY LEA

Hunting the Whole

Way Home

University Press of New England

Hanover and London

University Press of New England
Hanover, NH 03755
© 1994 by University Press of New England
All rights reserved
Printed in the United States of America
5 4 3 2 1
CIP data appear at the end of the book

ACKNOWLEDGMENTS

The author would like to thank the editors of the following periodicals, in which certain of these chapters—sometimes in slightly and sometimes in radically different form—first appeared: *Sports Illustrated:* "End of a Natural," "On the Lookout"; *The Southern Review:* "The Buzzards"; *The Valley News* (Lebanon, New Hampshire): "Summer"; *The Virginia Quarterly Review:* "A Winter Grouse," "Mercy on Beeson's Partridge," "A Track"; *The Cimmaron Review:* "Tutto nuovo"; *Prairie Schooner:* "Presences"; *The Georgia Review:* "Alone, with Friends," "On the Bubble"; *The New Virginia Review:* "Honesty."

"The Buzzards" was also published in *Fathers and Sons* (ed. David Seybold, Grove-Weidenfeld, New York, 1992).

The dedicatory poem originally appeared (as "Dedication") in my collection *The Floating Candles* (University of Illinois Press, Champaign, 1982). The poems that head each part of the book have also appeared in prior collections of mine, as follows: Part I: as "Sereno," in *No Sign;* Part II: under the title here used, in *No Sign;* Part III: as the title poem in *Prayer for the Little City* (Scribner, New York, 1990); Part IV: as "Fall," in *No Sign* (University of Georgia Press, Athens, 1987); Afterword: as "Museum," in *Prayer for the Little City.*

Lines from Wallace Stevens' poem "Esthetique du Mal" are from *Collected Poems* by Wallace Stevens. Copyright 1947 by Wallace Stevens. Reprinted by permission of Alfred A. Knopf, Inc., and Faber and Faber Ltd.

Excerpts from Robert Frost's poems "Hyla Brook," "Two Tramps in Mud Time," and "Does No One at All Ever Feel This Way in the Least?" are from *The Poetry of Robert Frost* edited by Edward Connery Lathem. Copyright 1936, 1944, 1952, © 1962 by Robert Frost. Copyright 1964 by Lesley Frost Ballantine. Copyright 1916, 1944, © 1969 by Henry Holt and Company, Inc. Reprinted by permission of Henry Holt and Company, Inc., and Random House UK Ltd.

The final poem was first published in *Wilderness* magazine as "Hunter's Sabbath: Hippocratic."

Late February. Orion turned
the corner into the long
sleep, blindness
on the earth's black side,
as you did.
Sleet. Cloud.
Woodsmoke creeping
like a whipped dog flat
to the ground, and heaven
was all occultation.
So the few last bitter lights,
down to Betelgeuse,
in familiar constellation—
they slipped away
before I'd caught the art
of naming. Early
fall now, now again
the wanderers—the winter
planets, memory, restless birds—
begin to shift. It will be greater
darkness if the language sulks,
unrisen. Flesh of my flesh,
you pause to take
quick breath
against the quick descent of evening.

I feel that exhalation
along the throat, I wear you
as I wear your threaded
hunter's coat, my father.
From which in this gust
into night there climbs
—like word or star—
a single feather . . .

CONTENTS

ON THE MARGINS

A Foreword

But yield who will to their separation,
My object in living is to unite
My avocation and my vocation
As my two eyes make one in sight.
Only where love and need are one,
And the work is play for mortal stakes,
Is the deed ever really done
For Heaven and the future's sakes.
—Robert Frost
"Two Tramps in Mudtime"

MOST OF THESE pieces were originally sent on assignment or speculation to magazines or newspapers. If when pieced together they approximate a book, then, its unity came about in a delightfully nonmethodical way, and spared me most of the usual occupational anxieties—is there a sustained argument, an overall structure, a sufficient array of particulars, a cohering point of view? I composed something here, then something there, and took no thought for the morrow.

Of course this nonchalance may have generated its own defects. Presented in a continuous format, a prose collection should indeed show thematic and narrative continuity, a distinguishing fabric of imagery, a shapeliness. I believe such criteria are satisfied here chapter by chapter; but without having construed any one of those chapters in relation to another, I worry that in gathering them I try to mask reiteration—of topic, figure, and even fact—as consistency.

Despite (or because of) all that, point of view has at least been no problem. Though in some cases undertaken at significantly different times from each other, these essays do reveal an enduring set of private obsessions, and thus perhaps my most honest version to date of "I." Not always gratified by that protagonist, I can't deny being interested in him. Like anyone, I'm curious about my own thoughts and emotions over a span of years, the concerns that once stopped me in my tracks, and that, subjected to meditation, turn out to have mattered so. But like anyone I'm also distracted enough by dailiness that such insights can prove surprising.

Writers, in doing what they do, often stumble on this sort of surprise. Indeed, I've always considered that one of their best *motives* for writing; we persist because we run into things we didn't know we felt, and in the process glimpse the foundations of our faiths and fears, morals and vices, hopes and despairs.

I frankly can't conceive of proceeding otherwise, keeping an eye for example on an editor's imaginable response, or even a reader's, much less on dim prospects like money or reputation. There are fine authors who can specifically choose their subject matter, or even their settings, and I don't mean to denigrate them; I'm simply not among their number, my subjects seeming always to choose *me*.

All this is closer to a confession of limits than a claim of virtue, since my own motives may in fact strike some as solipsistic. I take heart from the immanent genius of my neighborhood; bending an Horatian aphorism, Robert Frost once declaimed, "No tears in the writer, no tears in the reader," by which I think he meant that without his or her personal discovery an author's work will fizzle. (The dreariness of so-called Socialist Realism, with its aprioristic agenda, is perhaps the classic modern instance.)

We may of course be unpleasantly surprised by our self-discoveries, even to the point that we balk at publishing some of them, yet in the act of writing itself we are obligated to acknowledge them. That's what writing is for. And never mind certain voguish critical theory of the moment, with which I here and there quarrel, perhaps amateurishly, in what follows: the fact that authorial discovery, no matter how alien from a reader's own insights, is *shareable* accounts for such allegiance as real literature has always commanded. And will command: However darkly we're warned of a serious readership's diminishment, it will never truly vanish. There are those who won't accept a substitute for the power of the genuine, penetrating word.

Back, however, to private reckoning. In putting this collection together, I notice my ongoing struggle to make sense of a life. To say so is scarcely to confer distinction on individual essays, the book at large, or me—who doesn't engage in that struggle, as author and as person? Yet I hope that very distinction is false, because I trust in a continuity between my writing and all the other things that hold my closest attention: family affections, religious beliefs (uncanonical, and more implicit here than actively explored), hunting, dog handling, fishing, natural surroundings. While not excusing the repetitiousness I fretted over a moment past, such a trust does account for it. The relations of Then to Now, of child to parent and parent to child, even of this dog to that, this quarry to the next—for me, ideally, all these must fall into an integrity, and a book is a place for such integration to occur.

In my time there may remain no other place. Attitude toward place itself is of course central in each essay that follows—which too often, sad to say, means an attitude toward the *despoliation* of place. My feelings on such a matter are sometimes elegiac, sometimes furious, usually both; but they are entirely ungovernable. Given the things I write of, the things I do and love, the things on which I have based the quest to unify my experiences, I cannot edit the feelings out.

Rereading these essays, in fact, I almost comprehend the zeal of crusaders with whom I bitterly disagree. Though five times a father, I do not, for example, accept the guiding assumptions of the anti-abortionist—that even the earliest embryo has a right to life, that to deny it is therefore murder. But if I momentarily imagine I *did* accept these assumptions, I simultaneously imagine my own outrageous rhetoric and behavior on the issue. In the face of what one considers filthy crime, moderation itself seems criminal.

It is clear that I do cling to powerful—and maybe related—

premises. I will never articulate them so movingly as the great
Aldo Leopold, who proposed that land had *its* right to life; but
following his lead I insist that greedy violations of landscape
are . . . murder. This is not, however, an ideology tricked up to
protect my own backyard. As I write, to be sure, there's a vicious
scheme afoot to "develop" a gorgeous New England mountain
on which we have lived; but I can affirm in good conscience that
my hatred is no stronger for this ruinous plan than for the wreck
of a New Mexican or Siberian or Brazilian or Norwegian wildness.

Sin is sin.

My belief in the rights of wild place extends to wild *creatures* as
well. Since fair numbers of these pieces touch on hunting, that
posture may be perplexing to anyone but hunters themselves.
Though to some degree I write for these hunters, I hope also to
address open-minded nonhunters, a category that necessarily ex-
cludes the committed *anti*-hunter. I know from experience that
no advocates of so-called animal rights, whatever their position
along the movement's reasonable-to-kooky spectrum, will associate bloodsports with even so mild a term as conservation.

But let me explore that term's implications for other readers'
sakes. It is derived from the same root as our word "conservative," and—despite my lifelong allegiance to progressive
politics—one thing I also discover in these pages is how aptly the
conservative label fits me. It fits me, that is, if it means a person
who wishes to *save,* to hold *together,* who is concerned for what
I've called integrity. Like me, that person may find odd the
American right wing's persistent appeal to an ideal of unfettered
growth, one of whose catastrophic results is the vision of land as
mere real estate. (Just so, women have for too much of history
been viewed in a similar, proprietary manner; we speak eloquently
in referring to reckless subdivision or timbering or drilling as
rape.) I can imagine, say, the horror of a genuine conservative like
Edmund Burke at the worldwide sundering of rural cultures—
ancient and organic, but pitiably fragile—by this grotesque vision.

In my corner of the globe, it is not only the ladyslipper, the
woodcock, the indigenous trout, the black duck, the painted
trillium and countless other wild marvels that give way to the ski

condo, the mall, the office park; it is also a certain honorable way of reading the world. The genuine hunter or fisherman feels a Burkean revulsion at all this dislocation and pillage. No one knows better how the trampling of landscape's rights affects human community: the promised jobs for locals come and go, nature and human nature are split, and wild surroundings are flattened, in several senses, into one more wonderless zone. Forever.

All this in turn affects, even more irredeemably, the community of wildlife. No untamed species is threatened with diminishment, let alone extinction, by legal bloodsports; the unspeakable threat lies in the eradication of habitat, so often justified, precisely, by the imperatives of "growth." Unlike many of their detractors, then, true and worthy sportspeople are likely active in efforts to reject those imperatives, to sustain or restore the wild things' domains.

Note that I've just spoken of *true* and *worthy* sportspeople. It is, alas, impossible to deny the existence of other types. Whatever heat I feel for the misprision, misrepresentation, and general mischief of the organized anti-hunting lobby, it's nothing compared to my rage at those others. Slob hunters better pray I'm never in charge of their punishment. I'd make it a felony to apply the word "hunter" to themselves, even if modified by the adjective "slob." This book's periodic censorship of such thugs is as close to reasonable as I'll ever get.

But once again, in what follows my main objective is to discover and to convey *why* I feel the angers and raptures I do, and not in a facile way. If I reject the animal-rightist, I cannot then resort to the morally idiotic yap of the National Rifle Association and certain other "sportsmen's alliances," which can equal the frothy foolishness of a Cleveland Amory. My mission after all is as much artistic as philosophical; as I said at the outset, I hope I may reach people whose principal interest lies, simply, in an author's effort to write well. If nothing else, this must surely mean his avoidance of rhetorical shortcuts.

Tom McGuane, having gutted a Montana antelope, reflects that "this is goddamned serious and you better always remember that."

Exactly.

And the same applies to writing. One's aim in either case should be disciplined, steady, true.

For my purposes, of course, the hunter/author parallel cannot extend indefinitely. For one thing, I here occasionally address other pursuits than hunting, and for another—though I touch on subordinate successes—the primary standard for a hunt's success, like it or not, is a kill.

No such conspicuous standard existing for a writer's accomplishments, even in his or her own eyes, it seems impossible entirely to free the writing life of unease. If I started, for instance, by claiming that any relation among this book's parts was unplanned, I can't by that claim simply gloss over certain gaps in what follows. The reader will notice, for example, that the "I"— for all his insistence on the primacy of a kill—often deliberately stops himself from shooting, and unfailingly releases his fish. One could surmise (as I'll often do myself) that the protagonist dwells in states of marginality.

And yet all this is at least metaphorically appropriate: Prime cover for quarry tends to occur at edges, young growth giving way to old, relatively open terrain to dense, a vigorous flow to a gentle. Just so, "I" often finds himself between pure indulgence in narrative and a deep suspicion of any story, especially his own. There are moments for him when the connections, say, between Then and Now seem fictional in the very worst sense. No matter his search for resolution, integrity; all closure seems to give him pause. He may sniff at the trendy literary theorists who ascribe an irremediable indeterminacy to verbal constructs; yet how often I and "I" are prey ourselves to a chilling indeterminacy: We lower the gun rather than shooting the last grouse of a season. We leave conclusions cloudy, as if all the things to which we testify here were *too* damned serious—as often they are—for words alone.

Newbury, Vermont, 1993

I

Goodbye, Boy

Month when my cord to the womb was cut, yet almost hot
this wind, all strung with ducks, with Oldsquaw, Bufflehead,
and Whistler. And the ones I'm after—high,

The clever Blacks, who stretch their necks, and circle, and light
out of my range for good. There was a time
this might have prompted anger, and anger self-contempt:

What was I doing here, blue feet and fingers blocks like wood,
the very moisture of my eyes iced over, and icebergs in my blood?
My blood flows easier with age, the rage to question

Faltering. Like useless thoughts, the trash-birds strafe my blind.
My poor dogs whine: why does the gun stay silent?
Because, as I can't tell them—because I simply watch

The nobler ducks catch whiteness off the sun,
which grows these days each day more rare,
and the bay's best blue. Parade of change.

The wind from north is warm, is wafting
forgiveness here. To noble and ignoble.
Here on Frenchman's Cove on a spit of land, and blinded,

In this strangely torpid season I forgive
the bullies and the bullied, everyone and -thing
who wants to live, that wants to live,

The chasers and the chased:
the killer put to death today by pentathol injection,
far from here, in Texas;

I forgive the injectors;
I forgive the intractable shyness of all secrets,
like the ducks that stay far out of range.

I forgive all beings in their desperation:
murdered, murderer; mothers, fathers wanting something
that the children they bring forth can't give;

Myself for my own childhood cruelties—
the way I taunted Nick Sereno
(*serene*, a thing that neighbor never was,

Dark hungry victim, bird-boned butt of my deceptions . . .
the time I decoyed him out onto the raft
and cut him loose, and jumped.

I cut the frail hemp tether, and off he drifted, quacking fear).
And I forgive the fact that cruelty can circle:
grown, he paid me back in a steaming gin mill.

O, this balm of sun!
As if a lifetime's bruises might be balmed.
O, that summer would at last outlast the things to come!

Out on the flooding shellfish beds the Scoters pinwheel,
as if in fun and not in search of food.
I can even forgive the fighter pilots flying

Low as Harriers across the headland.
They flush the drifting Blacks in fear toward me.
In the hot breeze, I can count their single feathers,

Black and blue as birth,
with a seeming whiteness underneath.
Again my sweet-souled dogs look up, perplexed.

They champ their still undulled white puppy teeth.
There is more to all of this than I allow.
Here, in this paradox of weather—

Here for now I let things go,
the mind as light as light upon the wind,
as if here changed and changed into an answer.

The Buzzards

LOOKING ACROSS Swamp Creek from my grandparents' meadow, I could count on finding them. I'd seen one or two from close enough to know they weren't handsome. Yet I forgot that as I watched the simple ease of their drifting over the opposite ridge, so lovely I'd behold it for hours. Or more likely I *imagined* the passage of hours—all time moves lazily for a child on summer vacation; no doubt that's why I still associate the glide of vultures with a lost, languorous innocence.

My memories of the grandparents are vague, scattered: a snatch of talk here, a gesture or two there. They were gone early, and their house in Sumneytown, Pennsylvania devolved to my father. It has since passed on to others, and eastern megalopolis gulped its once wild surroundings. While Dad lived, however, it seemed a genuine backcountry retreat. Though the word didn't fit even then, we called it The Cabin.

My father's father had dammed Swamp Creek at the foot of his meadow before any of us grandchildren—three brothers, and, eventually two sisters—was born. We'd soak in the swimming hole till our fingertips wrinkled and blued. Then we would walk or paddle upstream, where the water ran through a great boulder field. Like all child societies, ours had a pecking order, and each family member or friend's position within it was established on The Rocks, as we artlessly called them. How rapidly could we improvise a way from this boulder to that? How wide were the chasms we dared to leap? Our play inevitably resulted in painful abrasions, but barring any worse injury, we'd carry on full speed till exhaustion overcame us.

Afterward we'd lie on a level slab we named Flatbed, from which we could also see those sailing buzzards. And as the rock warmed my bones and my breath slowed, I always imagined my father's presence, no matter where he physically was. I'd look through slitted eyes at the birds in their cycles, steady and effortless as earth's, and at length could imagine gentle revolution in my own being.

❧

I am the eldest son of an eldest son, and named for him. In remembering my father, I long to establish profounder symmetries than these obvious, factual ones; yet every effort feels instantly compromised by his early death. Sydney Lea, 1909–1966: to think of that terse message on his urn is to imagine the abrogation of some deep *formality* between us.

At over six feet tall and two hundred pounds, my father looked imposing. But his slowness to anger was almost perverse, or so I sometimes thought. Enjoying (the word is exact) a reputation for gentle judgment, he was also known for sympathy with players against long odds, from fellow businessmen down on their luck to the pioneer blacks, as I'm especially proud to recall, of the modern civil rights movement.

I associate my father most fondly with the outdoors. Unlike mine, his was never a character to be positively consumed by a passion for woods or waters or gun dogs. I confess I now and then held this against him too: If he insisted on doing so many other things with integrity, why be casual with these? In that much more calm and casual fashion, however, he loved these things I love, and he introduced me to them early. For this, at least, I am grateful.

Most of my reactions to his death proved a lot messier. Among them was a peculiar fury, as though this time tolerance had gone too damned far, the way for example it often had with an unruly dog; as though my father had given too much of his famous big heart. He should have shown who was boss. To whom? Well, to someone, even if that wasn't his style.

After the funeral, as I stood staring at a few nothings returned by the hospital staff—my father's watch; his ungainly steel pocketknife with the crescent wrench at one end; $1.09 in coin—I recognized terror in my responses too. Suddenly, at twenty-three, I was not only mortal but also unprotected: ever the hothead, I might curse my father's tolerance, but it had after all blessed me, however incompletely I'd felt the blessing till now. Inseparable from such feelings of deprivation, though, was another feeling, dim and painful at once: I was henceforth fated—a bit like Coleridge's sailor, but well before reaching his age—to tell a tale that would never be quite complete.

❦

It must be late summer of 1952, my mother big with her first daughter, my first sister. Why else would she stay at home? The two younger brothers are somewhere else too: I can't say where, or even care, my own wonderful circumstance crowding out such trivial detail. I've come to The Cabin alone with my father, a treat so rare that a noble truth about him has the freshness of discovery: he knows when and when not to be on hand.

Since breakfast, he's been working in the squat little smokehouse. The building lost its original function before I ever saw it, and is now a kind of guest quarters whose plaster needs whitewash. I haven't been asked to help. I've been set free to swim all these hours unattended. No other parents would leave me to such happy devices: They'd worry about drowning, or maybe even snakebite. My father is above such ignorance; like me, if more quietly, he holds it in some contempt. A father to be proud of.

At about 10:30 I dog-paddle—a fair swim and most of it over my head—to The Rocks; but I'm not inclined to play up there by myself. Instead I flop down on Flatbed to watch some half-dozen buzzards, riding the updrafts over Finland Ridge. Each follows each in a circle, the first one dipping out of sight on the far side, returning just as the last disappears. I close my lids when the lead buzzard drops behind the hill, and try to open them exactly when he sails back into view. Though the game works rather successfully for a spell, I finally shut my eyes and forget to reopen them.

Coming to, I blink, a feeling behind my brow telling me I've

dozed. The buzzards are still in the same formation. As I get to
my feet, a green heron startles me, squawkily flushing close by. It
lights in the brown ash above Serpent Rock, and I wonder if a
heron might eat a snake. I hope not. We like to peek into the
boulder's cleft, my brothers and I, because we can rely on finding
the snake at home. Although we often poke at the poor thing with
a stick, it never comes out, only hisses and jets its stink (which is
horrible but seems appropriate, almost attractive). My father
frowns on such play, explaining over and over that we court no
danger, as we prefer to think. Rather, we inflict terror on a
defenseless being, and ought to be ashamed.

On Flatbed, I feel a moment of soft breeze before I slide back
into water whose warmth by now so nearly matches the air's that I
scarcely notice the change. Invisible current carries me all the way
to the sluice in the dam's apron, where the usual tiny sunfish—
pumpkinseeds—nibble at my toes.

An ordinary day, then, but an extraordinary situation: How
fine it is to be half on my own, free at least of the younger brothers
who forever dog my steps at The Cabin. Not that I resent their
company; only that in its absence I can do as I want, undistracted,
all but a man.

Walking up through the meadow, flushing rackety grasshop-
pers, I discover that what I really want is food. Yet the sun's still
well east, and I sigh, knowing I'll have to wait out my father's
work. Having taken on his job, he will proceed with maddening
patience until it's done. I turn into the woods just shy of the
porch, making for the spring we call Frog Village.

How long must I stay there? Likely a good while. I forget
about my own hunger at any rate, forget even to expect the low
moan from the conch shell, my father's familiar summons back to
The Cabin—a sound so mellow and full of liquid glissandi that we
children always take our own sweet time responding to it.

It isn't the horn I finally hear, though. It's the fire-bell. I
stiffen. Nobody, adult or child, is allowed to ring that bell except
in emergency. For all the days I have spent here, I've heard it only
one time, when Uncle Roy's springer spaniel Speed was bitten by
a copperhead. I suddenly recall how frantic and frightened we
were, at least the children, piling into the wood-paneled Chevy,

Speed's paw swelling more grotesquely by the minute, the closest vet way off in Green Lane.

Breathless, I reach the Cabin, where I'm instantly relieved, and thrilled. My father takes me by the shoulders and steers my gaze across the swimming hole to an incredible descent of vultures to the top of the ridge.

He doesn't need to say anything. I gallop close after him over the field and the dam and up the hillside, so driven by wonder and curiosity that the quick climb seems easy. Still and all, my father is soon well ahead of me. When at last I duck under a soft, out-of-place willow and come through to the other side, he's already among the buzzards. Behind him I can just see the heavy-racked whitetail buck that has drawn them. Even in death the animal seems—self-contained. He's an unusual-looking deer, almost black, with a pure ebony strip from withers to flag. It's late summer, and the buck's antlers trail a grizzled rag or two of velvet, but by contrast to its coat the horns look phosphorescent, ghostly. The sun strikes his upside eye; it crackles like a sparkler.

A string of vultures perches in the evergreen stand at the far edge of the clearing. I sense more than see them, intent as I am on the fallen deer. And yet I feel somehow that the birds, too, are part of a composition whose foreground is commanded by my father. I want to enter the picture, and take a step or so in his direction, but he signals me back with a flatted palm. In the instant, my attention swinging to that big hand, I believe in his ability to arrange things however he chooses. In fact, I imagine that he has already done so, that in some way he keeps me off not for fear of my reactions but of disturbing an exquisite rightness, the balance he has willed into being. The deer at my father's back, larger than any I've seen, is small compared to him. Even the vultures' high hemlocks shrink as I look on.

Though I know in my soul that the buzzards will have at the dead buck again, which is as it should be, it's a *stasis* that will linger in mind for years: My father, turning, raises his arms like a prophet; the buzzards take to air in their hundreds, climbing and climbing till at last they resume their slow cycles in the sky, full of familiar grace.

❧

Here's another version:

My father and I are the only ones here, and he's been busy. He still is. I can picture him in his baggy, whitewash-spattered shorts, cooking inside The Cabin. Alone and bored all morning, I'm looking forward to lunch as a relief, however temporary or minor. Why must everything take so *long*? The frogs are stuffed: I've caught one bug after another for them, and they've lost interest. I watch the surviving mayflies kick and twitch, and I wait for the honk of the shell.

When I hear the porch-bell instead, I don't think to worry. I think: Something's up. I come in a rush, low softwood limbs abrading my face. But there isn't any disaster waiting. Dad's pointing at Finland Ridge, where the buzzards are thick as roost-bound crows.

"Let's go see," he says, his eyes shining the way they do, sometimes over the smallest matters. He makes for the dam at a kind of dogtrot.

I've watched vultures land on the ridge often enough, but never, it's true, in numbers like this. As I catch up with my father, I catch up with a little of his enthusiasm too.

The woods on the far side of the creek are dense in any season, but especially summer. They make slow going, and it's a hot, hard climb up the flank. When I pause for breath in the clearings, I can see straggler birds luffing down through the canopy at the spot we mean to reach. But the spot doesn't seem to get closer; I begin to feel that it's actually *receding* as we move. My small excitement fades, and I also begin to feel like quitting. I whip my poor body on, though, trying to believe in a purpose beyond the mere discovery of what some vultures are up to. Trying to believe this is what's called man's work.

At last I crawl under a cedar, scratching my face again on dry lower limbs, and my palms and knees on the spills. When I straighten up, I see the full flock. It's a huge, black, filthy swirl, my father standing on this side of it, his shirt soaked, his mouth gapped for air, his glasses clouded with steam. He looks balder than I remember, dumpier.

It's a long spell before I can take my eyes off him. Winded as he is, he keeps trying to light a smoke, but his hand shakes and he drops his Zippo again and again. When he finally goes down on his knees to grub for it, I look away to the buzzards. They're swarming a cowhorn deer, its little tines crusty with old velvet, its hamstrings ruined. Dogs, I figure. We don't have any other predators to manage the job. Is it those rotted hindparts I smell, or the birds themselves? I'm surprised by the *sound* of the vultures, something between a hiss and a hoot, like barn owls on a rafter. At this close distance, their sheer ugliness also surprises. And how much smaller they seem than I've imagined!

Young as I am, I've been a hunter for two years and seen a fair amount of blood; yet the sight of the young deer, maimed by the dogs and now by the buzzards, revolts me. To think of its suffering! Couldn't it have outrun a pack of fat pets? I retreat some. So does my father; but when he reaches my side he suddenly appears to have second thoughts and walks unsteadily back toward the carcass. Sure enough, like their Hollywood cousins, the vultures hop only a few yards off. They shoot their necks and gawk; they hiss and cluck. I don't know what my father's designs are, either on bird or buck. I don't really want to know.

Scrambling and tumbling down the hillside, I fetch up at the dam. Directly south, the sun turns the color of a tin cup, and I feel the first drops of gray, tepid rain. It's only a minute or so before my father joins me. His chest is still heaving, and he doesn't say a word. Holding his fogged eyeglasses in one hand, he squints along the apron for a few moments, then, feeling with his soft moccasin soles—as one might do to cross a room in pitch dark— he walks to the other shore, a step at a time.

I follow. Both of us silent, I can hear the silly gabble of the buzzards, feasting in the high woods. To block the noise, I start to whistle tunelessly. The swimming hole is scantly pocked by the rainfall; at the sluice, the usual trash fish—bluegills and sunnies— face me just under the surface, rounding their white-rubber maws, hoping for a crust, or even a crumb.

In our absence, the hamburgers have gone gelid and beady, and in any case we are short on appetite. My father scrapes the meat into a paper bag, to be dropped off at the dump on the way home, then wanders into his bedroom. Soon his irregular snores sound from behind the door.

Left on my own, I take up a Red Ryder comic book. I read the accounts of Red's triumphs, first to myself in silence and then again and again, louder and louder—stressing each *pow!* and *bang!*—as if to wake my father.

⚜

Now, almost forty years later, I'm lugging my five-year-old son in a backpack up the steepest side of Stonehouse Mountain, New Hampshire. It's the middle of June, a gorgeous day, the leaves the size of a fox's ear, the woods going green out of gold. He likes to pretend we're after game to feed us through a season, so we'll be bushwhacking through good cover for an hour or so, and we'll keep hunting the whole way home.

There are no buzzards here, old or new; but there is a boy. He has so much ahead of him now, and I so much behind. Yet there are other and brighter auguries too: I'm in damned good shape— a lot better, I suspect, than my father was at this age, just a decade short of his death—and I'm lucky to have so much splendor outside my very door, pure in its different way as the beauty around The Cabin, before the changes.

I've labored for thirty minutes to reach this ledge. We call it Flying Squirrels because once, in winter, we flushed a crowd of the things from a holey white pine at its top. Their soaring was a wonder, carrying them clean out of sight down the flank of the mountain. Thus, as places sometimes will, this one now strikes us as almost sanctified. If the squirrels have never been seen again, still the spot remains rich with promise as well as recall.

But I summon myself back to matters before me. My burden is precious, I must take care, I will pick my way with both hands and feet here. When I grasp the final outcropping and pull us onto height-of-land, I nearly touch the fawn who lies in a stone hollow. As it jumps and goes, I can almost feel my little son's eyes widen behind me. "Look!" he bellows. "Look! Look! *Look,* Dad!"

The fawn bounds north along the monolith. Reaching the drop-off, it poses side-to. Perfect, all this: dark evergreen in the near distance, four pale rivers of lingering snow on Mt. Moos-ilauke in the far, the music of deepwoods birds all around us, and the smell of new mud and fern. We watch for another few mo-ments before the little deer steps gingerly back our way, close enough that its white spots come into focus again. We see its delicate nostrils, flared by caution. Then it bolts, leaping a juniper clump and dashing down into black swamp eastward.

I clamber on a few feet, and stop. We hear the rustle and splash of the small beast's going, and at length the bleating of the unseen doe as she searches it in the brush. Nothing and no one around me is really dead. The child on my back will ride me till we're home. My chest heaving, my glasses fogged, I stand till he urges me on. I suppose someday he'll want to tell the story of this scene—and of his father's part, or parts, in it.

Hard Hands, Soft Moon

N O WAY, OF COURSE, to be sure those sea-run brown
trout would have taken the fly. But it does look good,
sailing into the brush. I fling the whole box of size
eighteen hooks after it, turn around and scream: "This is the
worst fishing trip ever!"

Years back, that bass—biggest I'd ever had on a line—charged
under the rowboat and snapped off. My tears were furious.

"It isn't a fishing trip. It's our honeymoon." She's succinct, not
truculent.

I want to do things my own way: Unsure what might hatch in
Spain, I packed my streamside vice, a range of dubbing material,
and one of the Darbees' dun necks, so that I might tie what I
needed, right on the spot. I am made chiefly of the lust for
success, especially with fish and game; the young woman's com-
posure therefore enrages me. That these Orvis hooks are lemons,
every one of their eyes pinched and unthreadable, is bad enough.
That my new wife should keep blithely and irreverently casting
her size twelve Tupp's and should even land several of the heavy-
toothed, deep-bodied, slurping trout is intolerable.

Why not look up and notice the skill and ardor of bats, hear the
nightly gong from the abbey, of which nothing remains but the
bell tower itself? Why not take pleasure in the smell of residual sun
in the stones, still warm on the bank? Why not think back just a few

days, when in a single weekend I netted seven beautiful Narcea salmon, including that luminous 25-pounder?

It is 1966, I am twenty-three, and I pledge to boycott Orvis forever. (I won't actually honor my vow till a few years later, when the catalogue begins to include more wraparound skirts and cufflinks than outdoor gear.) I whip a sapling with my Leonard rod. I curse the very neighborhood goats, who seem to snicker from the waterside path.

Although these Iberian ephemerids are something like our Infrequens, their fitchy shade has an odd *glint*. I'm prepared, however, having brought along a spool of silver wire that makes the adjective "fine" seem coarse.

Where'd I get this stuff? Maybe from that mail-order outfit in Michigan, the one that stiffed me five bucks for the wood duck fibers they never sent, the crooks.

The fly I've tossed away was sparely ribbed with the wire. In flight, it caught the inchoate moonlight just so. Yes, were I a trout on inland tour, I at least would have leapt at such a thing. Now I must resort to a pale upright, dressed to mid-June Battenkill specs. Hell, though, it looks ludicrous, looks bigger than it is.

Below the covered bridge in West Arlington, that twenty-incher gulped my Hendrickson and ran into a muskrat hole. God, the tricks they'll pull! I actually hated that fish.

Of course this Vermont dun might work if I genuinely wanted it to; but I thrash the water, as if to show the gods what an impossible hand they've dealt. It plain won't *do* to catch a fish.

My wife, knowing me, knows also not to chide, nor to whoop when she nets another thick trout. I crash back up to the rented Peugeot, muttering over my shoulder that it's late, that we face a long trip to our next hotel, in the ancient city of Avila. From the road, I yet hear the *whoomp* of rising browns, the fish I'll prefer, lifelong, to any other. The hell with a salmon.

You're young and relatively poor, and you get to the damned
Miramichi just as the heat wave hits. The water goes to eighty
degrees, and you beat it vainly, angrily.

But at length my mood lightens, not least at the prospect of
Avila, one of whose medieval rulers forebade the spending of
more than half a given year's budget on troubadours. My own
poetry is as yet unremarkable and unremarked, but I dream
naively of improving it just by visiting a place where the art
seemed once so crucial.

How lovely the countryside, after all! The aura of moon becomes moon itself, breaking over the Sierras to eastward. How
lovely my girl-bride, her face open, unduly forgiving. It is nine
o'clock. There'll be a late Spanish supper—unpretentious food, a
draft of vintage, intimate small talk—and then a room overlook-
ing the walled town.

Behind us lies the much smaller town of Crado. In the rearview
I see its light rising to diffuse itself in the sudden lunar brightness.
Ahead, a boar crosses the road; then a fox.

Never mind that the run of hooks was defective. That hatch was
perversely copious, the fish big: I have squandered all that, but
never mind. Crado wasn't so bad, really. The recollected taste of
the hotel's blood oranges stings the place where my jaws meet; the
vista from our bedroom was sublime; sweetness from the garden
below hung on our bedclothes at dawn.

I have no right to self-pity. Perhaps I get part of an important
insight: infuriating experience may in time cede to calm, may even
become savory in retrospect. I can't know that I'll learn this more
completely by virtue, precisely, of fishing; nor that calm may
eventually have a preemptive power too. If I'll only let it.

God damn! This fork in the road doesn't show on the map.
Easy, I tell myself. What were you just thinking? There: the
mountain range is still to eastward; right is still south, the way to
be heading. And all around, rustic families make their bizarre
crepuscular promenades. I'll cruise along for a bit, and then, if still
in doubt, trot out rudimentary Spanish, ask directions.

That twenty-five pounder thundered up the brawling Narcea till I saw spindle on the reel. Then it raced back down in a far channel on the other side of a bridge abutment. At casual risk to my life

—I shudder some now at the wheel—

I plunged in, waders and all, swimming across, holding my rod high. Gathering slack on the opposite shore, I thrilled to feel the salmon still there. The chef in Cornellana would dot the steaks with coarse salt, broil them over oak coals, bring them to our table with fresh greens.

"Where are we?"
"I'll ask," I reply, the road having turned to dirt without my notice.
The Spanish father draws four small daughters about him, as if protectively, but his answer is clear and courteous; the other fork after all—drive six kilometers, then bear left. An hour only to Avila.
I lean out of the Peugeot: "Muchas gracias." The peasant bows, the children titter.
The road grows wide and accommodating again.
Then it's dirt, but still broad.
Then dirt, but narrow.
Then a path.

And couldn't ever find that loaded brookie hole again, back in the woods. Washington County, 1957, year of the killer mosquito.

Seeing a burro ahead, jacked in its tracks by the headlights, I back out, ask another walker, whose family hides among pines.
"Oh no, *señor*, back toward Crado, but turn *right* at the highway—a simple hour to Avila. Very beautiful, grand."
"Muchas gracias," I say. The man inclines his head.

I could simply have gone down a size; the twenties were perfectly fine. Why not? Because I'm pigheaded and spoiled, my purism ruinous, manic. Every cast needn't put Kreh to shame. My every fly doesn't have to rival Whitlock. Even Homer nodded: every sonnet need not be "When in disgrace . . . ." Fish. Write. The world is all before you.

Before me now, however, another burro, wide-eyed in the high beams. Families scurry into the roadside brush like rodents. Through the open window, I hear their sibilant chat and laughter. I'll drive to the best road I can find behind us, keep the moon-bathed Sierras on my right, tending ever south. It has been two hours now, but Avila must be nearby. And those hours have been pleasant, maybe even instructive,

> the moon turned to the color of that fine silver rib on the discarded fly. I imagine it, cocked on its stiff hackle: the tinsel winks in the gleam amid flowery bushes. I could wish to be a painter. But it isn't bad to be what I am. In childhood, the willow boughs gobbled my crude home-made streamers, or occasionally a fish did . . . and broke off. I'd huff out of the woods, the biting insects strafing me, my brow a mess of sweat and cobweb. So life has indeed kept turning brighter since.

She has fallen asleep in the other seat, and she's better than I deserve, by far. Her hair trails out the window, and the moon capers on it.

I am unusually cool when the tire goes flat—unpack our fishing gear from the trunk with deliberation, trouble to read instructions on the jack, make the change. After Avila, there's another river to the north, and we've reserved a beat. There will be trout in my world forever.

I further astonish myself on hearing the crinkly sound under the Peugeot's back wheel. By God, I *am* being rational: I realize that if I hadn't run over my flyrod, I'd have driven away, abandoning it where I put it while removing the spare from the car's trunk. You only take one honeymoon, I tell myself (wrongly, but I won't know that for years): I'll just buy some cheap rod in Avila, whose soft lights now rise in columns, much as Crado's did.

And do. For this, clearly, *is* Crado. I have driven in a great circle.

How can it be that—having consistently kept those mountains (surely the Sierras) off to my right—I have arrived where I started, at the very place where I threw an eyeless mayfly imitation into the brush three hours ago? I've meanwhile crushed my Leonard eight-footer with a car, whose steering wheel I now twist, with a strength that age will mercifully sap, till it breaks in my hand.

☙

Hard hands in a soft moon. I can see them even now, a quarter-century later. They had yet to learn the full story, yet to learn gentleness. I would have to stroke my children's heads. I would have to draw a fish back and forth in current till it regathered vigor and swam off into memory, in which realm I might better comprehend the meaning of calm.

Goodbye, Boy

ON A CERTAIN MORNING last autumn, I spread my decoys offshore from Grant Balch's pasture. Such a gesture seems almost perverse nowadays, the degeneration of late fall waterfowling on this stretch of the Connecticut River having been catastrophic. If once I could blame a failed duck hunt on a boyish restlessness or bungling, now I can generally blame the simple absence of game. I've become a better retriever trainer, a better duck caller, and a better shot over the years—years that locally reduce these skills to near irrelevance.

Too soon old, too late smart, as they say.

One temptation is to stay in bed, since I might often kill as many ducks from there as from my blind. And yet I continue to go, drawn by the season and the hour. Bumping along in the ruts, my old retriever's head in my lap, my old canoe snubbed in the truckbed, I tune in a particular French Canada radio station; it features archaic rural fiddlers, and comes through clearly before the great interference machine of contemporary life cranks up— hard rock and soft, phone calls and faxes, dismaying news.

By noticing whose lights are on in the village, I can make a crude but authoritative demographic survey, which, to be sure, tells its own dismaying yarn. As the country people perish or are supplanted by refugee professionals, fewer and fewer kitchen lamps shine at 4:30 A.M. After his eighty-odd years, Grant himself is gone. As I drove to that morning's hunt, it was therefore a small reassurance to look through the window and return the wave of his wife Margaret, already at her coffee.

It was likewise fine to see Herefords still in her pasture, no matter that they belonged now to a neighbor. I even rather enjoyed my usual game at the gate: shooing the steers, then racing to get the truck through before they could regroup and race through too, the other way. The one with the scarred shoulder nibbled like a goat at my jacket as I restrung the barbed wire. Finished, I turned and ruffled the thick mane on his boss. We like that.

At river's edge, there was also the plain gratification of being in a beautiful place when the sun first comes to it, a white stain seeping down the high palisade on the Vermont side opposite. The shouts of unroosting crows jostled memories of my boyhood self, crouching in weeds near a papier-maché owl, hoping to outsmart what I then considered the wariest animal on earth. I'd seen so many warier ones since that that old headiness seemed nearly unimaginable. Yet I could and did imagine it after all, together with the pure, youthful compulsion to what I then called success.

Ducks or no ducks, I knew there'd be incidental blessings in this lovely reach of river. When hadn't there been? That astonishing eagle, studying my decoys from a young elm's branch ten feet above my head. That mink who ambled through the blind, climbing nonchalantly over my booted feet. That huge buck who swam from Vermont virtually into the same blind. Graceful passing of countless herons. Comic carryings-on of hooded mergansers— "little dippers," in local parlance—which always drive Topper, my ornithologically indiscriminate retriever, to distraction.

I could reasonably look forward to such possibilities; yet recent dawns on the river have left less room for prospects than for retrospects. Compared to other pursuits, of course, this was always so, even back when the shooting was hot. The mere job of busting brush for grouse precludes much soulful study until the sun itself is done. The same, for me, with chasing deer: I'm not made right to linger on stand; I must keep moving and pausing, moving and pausing, a method oddly called still hunting. But it's in a waterfowl blind that I do the only hunting that could rightly be so called. Physically stationary, however, I'm provoked to mental travel; and the fewer the ducks, the farther my range.

The morning I speak of, mild and windless, would have been unducky even in better days. Not that the real cold was so far off: snow buntings plucked at the cattails around me; juncos, flashing that shock of white tail, bounced by every few moments; one nervous gang of pine siskins simultaneously lit and flushed at pasture's edge. I watched a gray squirrel dash from his hole in a moribund pine, dash through a hawthorn hedge to Grant's stubbled corn piece, dash back with a full cheek; he knew what was at hand, and he meant to be ready for it.

A generous chunk of time passed until, away to the east, invisible even in the clear daylight, I heard a flock of geese tending southward. First over Mt. Cube. Then Smart's Mountain. Somewhere near Cummings Pond, I judged, they faded from hearing. Not long ago in this country, we'd have considered them late in migration. But everything changes. It was once a rarity in *any* time of year to see a few Canadas on a back pond or slough, not to mention on the river itself; now they've become almost common, and they stay longer. The majority are still high-flyers, headed for richer farmland, balmier climate, and it's still for the most part a pretty vain undertaking to hunt them over decoys. Yet there are those who've begun to do so, and the jump-shooters encounter greater success every season.

Some speculate that the Canadas, who already short-stop inland as far north as Massachusetts, will one day stop up here, too. Our winter months seem less and less frigid, often leaving patches of open water, so it does seem conceivable that geese will someday linger year-round in local grainfields (if in fact such fields themselves endure). Perhaps like the birds themselves, who now thrive on such upland fare rather than stuff from the vanishing marshes, I'll adapt to the change: I will refinish the honker decoys that have mouldered since I quit traveling to the Eastern Shore; I will brush up my rusty hail call and gabble; I will start hunkering in pits instead of brush blinds. With those geese flown on, it was easy to ponder all that; but it was hard to *feel* any of it, so different from everything I'd learned to expect.

Was the expectable, however, an automatic virtue? In a way, of course, yes, and my being on that rivershore proof enough. I'd come because this is what I do in that season, part of one autumn merging with its counterpart the next. On the other hand, what would hunting be without a mix of the expected and its utter opposite? That eagle; that mink; that deer; and just then—as if on cue—the watersnake who glided into a pond-lily cluster shoreward of my decoys. Warm though it was, who'd have figured to see such a creature even in a mild November? And indeed, the pretty little thing seemed languid, almost desperately so. When I stood for a better look, he slid off the rotted pads as slowly as a gorged alligator from a mudbank, cruising the surface to another batch a few yards downriver.

Topper watched the snake go, then looked around at me, quizzical. I rubbed his muzzle, clown-white with age, but he suddenly jerked from under my hand. As so often, I followed his stare to birds, though not this time to airborne ones. A pair of drake wood duck, who should long since have been gone from this territory, was paddling in among my blocks; lost in reminiscence and morose prophecy I'd missed their arrival.

Topper's trembling was strenuous yet controlled. Briefly rolling his eye back; as he does for example whenever the little dippers cavort unmolested before us, he mutely questioned me: For God's sake, will you *shoot*?

Just then I mutely answered: No.

The ducks were no more than a dozen yards off by now, the sun dazzling their crests, their inverted reflections exact in the pondlike water.

"Get out of here," I said in a speaking tone.

And out they got, their wake a lather of bubbles that caught the sunlight too. For a moment in flight, hard-edged and clean, the woodies appeared almost stationary against the Vermont cliff. But soon enough they became southerly specks. Only then did Topper relax, his body going loose in a huge, whining sigh.

"They looked too pretty," I mumbled. I could tell as usual that the dog disagreed, and I felt bad for him. A major motive for these unpromising duck expeditions, after all, was my hope of giving Topper some work. However fine his condition, he was ten years old, and he hadn't had a chance to show half his stuff for half his life. There's never been a lovelier pet than he, and I had long loved him in that part; but it wasn't the part his breeder had in mind, nor the one I'd rehearsed him for myself, from a puppy. Probably I should have tumbled at least a single. Too late for that.

Five years earlier, after watching his brilliant retrieves from a Chesapeake cove, a waterfowl outfitter had offered me an immense pile of cash for my dog. I don't miss that money, but to this day I wonder whether I shouldn't have made the deal, granting Topper a more appropriate life.

Yet how appropriate those *ducks* had been to the spangled glaze of the Connecticut.

Downstream a half-mile, Bernard Tullar's milking machines abruptly quit. Their drone is always so much a part of morning there that I never notice it till it's gone. Had an older man once sat in my place, brooding in his own way? Conscious of all that cow-barn mechanism, did he think back on a time when a dairy was more hands-on and human? Maybe. If so, it's unlikely that he'd ever hooked up a milking rig in a mid-winter dawn, any more than I have; and yet, if woods and waters both empower your psyche and exert power over it—if you *need* them as my visionary man and I do, along with their wild denizens—then you'll believe that the primary, tactile experience is at least as important as human convenience. Lacking such belief, who but a madman would be where I was in that November daybreak?

And yes, I had arrived at Grant's field in a four-wheel drive truck, its radio playing tunes from across national borders. I took full advantage of a mechanical epoch, which frees us in many ways, which provides us with mobility, which may protract our lives. Still, sometimes I wonder, where is it we will go, and what (to use the ready pun) is the *nature* of our health and our liberty? I'd rather travel a few splendid miles than many a gray one.

Or so I'll often say. My more honest self recognizes the delusion or at least the fecklessness of such nostalgias. Thus I've lately tried to convince myself that under new circumstances I might see through a new lens. Shouldn't that be possible? If the geese are to supplant the ducks, for example, why not be a goose hunter? Failing to adjust, I'll know a future devoid of anything *but* retrospection, banal and bitter at once. Looking back on that morning at Grant's, for instance, I might easily write, "the skies remained empty," when in fact they were full of motion and light, and even a stoic fall music: all around me, the brave calls of chickadees, just starting to arrive in real winter numbers; from crags on the palisade, the gritty croaks of ravens, scouting for road kill; deep in Grant's evergreens, the pileated woodpecker's flourish.

Why should I be less enthralled by any of these creatures than by a game bird? My answer is scarcely recondite, yet few will grasp it who have not traveled my kind of beautiful miles. And of course, indifferent or plain hostile to genuine hunting, that's exactly what most people will never do. I preach to the small choir. To the great congregation my sermon is either an atten-uated frontier romanticism or, more commonly, a bloodthirst tricked up as aesthetics.

It's true enough that I can't evade the fact of blood. A kill *defines* the hunt and all its subordinate objectives and agents, including the hunter: in that one moment, the path of an elusive and superbly equipped prey intersects with a human predatory capacity, both schematic and intuitive, mundane (which boots to bring, which shells?) and superstitious (hunt high ground in an east wind); and for that one moment, the world reveals a gor-geous coherency.

The anti-hunting propagandist is appalled by such a sacramen-tal perspective, precisely because its icon is a bloodstain. Nor will the hobbyist sportsman read me rightly. I speak only to and for the passionate hunter, the one who regards this business as more than mere sport. Surrounded like everyone by a mechanized and abstractive culture, he appreciates how seldom human gesture can be unmediated, literal.

I've always understood all this somewhere in my soul, but I've needed to come this far before bringing it to articulation, how-ever imperfect. Ironically, I worry that such a development may threaten the hunt's very value: if I ever reach a point of rational, self-conscious understanding, then the passional foundation of what I do will have vanished, along with its aesthetic. And its ethical foundation as well, even as vulgarly understood: the fact of blood will no longer mark an unmediated moment; however difficult of achievement, a kill will degenerate into cold-blooded *killing;* at long last I'll be forced to give this dear game up.

None of this has actually happened yet, and I pray it shall not;

but I can't deny that certain things do come clearer with age. For example, I understand why with every passing season hunting should seem a greater treasure than fishing, even if I'd not gladly sacrifice either. It's partly of course that hunting is the more fragile resource: I'll be physically able to fish well after I'm all done with hard terrain and icy blinds. But there's more to it than that. Conservation instincts, or plain common sense, dictate that we release the trout, the salmon, and even the bass we now catch. Thus the gesture of angling is ever more symbolic, less what I call a primary act than somehow a charade of the primary. I might say that hunting is to contemporary sportfishing roughly as the dead black duck at my feet is to the photo of him I might have taken instead. A direct, an undiluted *presence* on the one hand, and on the other a kind of disembodied *re-presentation*.

My craving for the former may seem odd. A writer's traffic is after all in words, and nothing (except perhaps money) could be more abstract or representative. But doesn't a northerner now and then lust for an untracked beach, a sun straight overhead, blue waves wheezing on the shingle? Doesn't he dream that in paradise he'll travel back and forth between such a southern place and the evergreen-dense hills behind the house that he's chosen for his own? My very commitment to a verbal and meditative art may quicken desire for similar vacation, one impulse galvanizing another. If I give words to my vision now, it was without them that it transpired—complete with the northman and the tropical sunlight, the white strand and the hillside house—on the morning I speak of. I remember it well.

Yet even as I remember and write, I must smile at myself. Though I hope that somewhere, sometime such contradictions may disappear, who besides me would all but leave his body in order to ponder the joys of unadorned physicality, would claim the benefits of primary pursuits while elaborating a billowy inward picture of some Eden-to-come? I am tempted to pun on the fact that I was in a blind that morning.

In any case, I hadn't the time for self-irony just then, for my reverie was broken by Topper's romping out of his crouch. I started to hiss him back under cover, but what the hell? There wouldn't be any ducks. Why not put the poor guy at his ease for a spell? Besides, it was getting toward the hour for gathering up decoys. I had projects waiting for me on my desk, and too extensive a voyaging into mental places always entails the risk of not getting back all the way.

The twittering of songbirds, the lisps of the breeze, and the faint hum of the river's current had by now become a sort of silence . . . through which to my amazement, off to northeast above Grant's stubblefield, pumped five soundless geese. It couldn't be, I thought, at the same time wondering if I'd ever beheld even a single Canada in such utterly soundless flight. I didn't believe so; still don't. The big birds were well up, and the sun shone frankly upon them. Like the wood ducks earlier, they appeared chiseled, lapidary; but they were moving, right enough—my way, their wings already set.

Surely they'd make one lofty pass over my spread and then travel on, even higher. I didn't of course have a Canada call. I was half out of the blind to boot, and Topper all the way out, bulling through the cattails, on furlough. He hadn't noticed the geese, who remained stone-quiet. And still came straight on.

I'd frozen in a semi-upright posture, imagining the sun's blaze off my balding head, the all-too-human angles and divots of my silhouette.

The geese kept incredibly coming.

I whistled once, curtly. At the signal Topper immediately sat, his hind parts in several inches of cold riverwater. Not that his caution or mine would do any good. By now the birds had certainly spied us: they'd squawk and flare in another few yards.

They flew ever toward us, mute.

The small flock broke the vertical plane of my set and abruptly dropped to the water outside it, facing the breeze. I took the moment to reseat myself. What few geese I'd ever seen in the Connecticut's actual water while hunting over decoys knew how to navigate the river's center, exactly out of shotgun range from either side. These five would of course be no different; they'd swim a half-dozen yards or so further offshore to get it just right.

But no: they turned and sculled in among my blocks, un-hesitating, unperturbed, one even dabbling the bar on which at daybreak my canoe had momentarily run aground. I could still see the frail keel-mark in the mud. Topper flattened, his whole belly and chest in the water now. Again his eye rolled toward me in its socket, and again I knew what he was thinking: Shoot, you fool!

But I wouldn't. Not yet anyhow.

I watched for a long spell. There seemed to be a couple of shortneck geese and three longnecks. Two married couples, I figured, and one bachelor or widower. I looked at Topper's clown face, then back at the gaggle. I was trying to determine which were the mated pairs so that I might kill the odd gander out, so that my dog could have *his* defining moment. But my thoughts grew ever more fussy and ludicrous: I recalled a chapter from Lorenz about homosexual goose matings. They lasted for life too.

"Get out of here," I declaimed for a second time.

Now the birds made racket enough, hauling their heavy bodies into air, lashing the slick to froth. My dog jumped instantly to all fours, his ears cocked, not shivering from the chill alone. We followed the Canadas out of sight to southward as we had the woodies.

Topper expelled another great breath, bigger than the earlier one. I broke my gun, unloaded it, and laid it on the dew-sopped vegetation behind me. Then, dropping to a knee and calling his name, I threw both arms around the old retriever's marsh-rank neck. He deserved my apology, had deserved it a long time. And yet shooting a single one of those geese would have been a sin: the word still seems precisely right.

It wasn't the birds' beauty and grace, nor their conformity to the land- and riverscape—even more stunning than the ducks'— that had dissuaded me. Or at least none of these things entirely. It was simply that I'd exercised no skills; rather, the game had atypically failed to exercise *its* skills, its keen senses, its native wariness. A kill, so far from defining anything, would have done just the opposite, ratifying the accidental, the random. It would have left me no better than the oaf who, driving by in his car, blasts a grouse off a roadwide wall, shooting merely because he's happened on something shootable. Or I'd have been the fool who, looking for deer, murders the bear he blunders across. In a child we may partly forgive such moral idiocy, but not an adult.

I had done the right thing. There could be no earthly doubt

about it. But I was suddenly overcome by an exquisite melancholy. My logic blamed this blueness on the double disappointment of an aged retriever, but something in my spirit resisted the neatness of that explanation.

By now the sun had melted the thin skin of frost on which my canoe slid so easily at dawn. I tried to drag the boat back to the truck with all my gear stashed in its hull, but could not. I needed to make several trips, fetching my decoy bags, my canvas stool, my gun, my shell bag and the rest. Yet even the weight of an empty boat seemed enormous in my state, which had turned to genuine depression, for reasons I still couldn't name. To name them, I'd have to wait till much later, and in order to make a cautious truce with that morning's emotions, I'd have to discover their relations to some prior emotions.

It seems that for me one retrospect begets another.

❧

Back in the 1960s, I once sat on a shore near the ice-wrecked bridge in Haverhill. That was far upstream from Grant Balch's pasture. It was also a much earlier fall day than the one at Grant's, so the teal hadn't left yet. A bird shy of a limit, and full of youthful avarice, I was waiting well into morning for a straggler.

All of a sudden I heard a pair of near Canadas, who before I knew it had passed outside my decoys and dropped about a hundred yards downstream. After they coasted around a bend, I leapt from the blind and ran after them, my heart a hammer. As I've said, a goose on ground or water was a spectacle in those days.

I tried to judge the distance these two might have swum, hoping they'd strayed closer to shore in the process. In that stretch, the riverbank on the New Hampshire side stands twenty feet or so above the Connecticut's flow; I might just be able to rush to a brink and—if I'd guessed properly—fire my gun. I'd been running along in a punishing half-crouch, and was badly winded; yet my body felt more than ever *alive*.

When I made my dash across a cut hayfield to streamside, I found I'd misestimated. Not by much, to be sure: had I scampered on another twenty yards, the birds would have given me a pretty decent shot. Indeed, if they hadn't in that uncanny way remained dead-center even in this skinny run of river, I'd still have had a reasonable one. As it was, they lifted off to north, honking, well out of harm's way.

I wasn't surprised, but I was surely disappointed. Or rather, resentful. Like any boy, I vaguely believed the world blameworthy for not accommodating my every craving. Back at the blind, I forgot all about the last teal I'd been wishing for. I jerked the canoe from the cattails and churned out to my spread, where I yanked the blocks on board, half willfully tangling line and anchor so that I could fume and curse even more bitterly.

For weeks and months after, I replayed the whole scene, but supplied a fantasy ending: Monster, my duck dog in those days, presented me with the first trophy, then proudly swam for the second; next came the labor of picking the birds, the pleasure and ardor of cooking them—a jigger of orange liqueur in the stock, shoots of celery in the birds' cavities, wild rice steaming on a top burner. The works.

❧

I compare the breathless, exhilarated pursuit of the geese by a man in his twenties with my almost comic deliberation at Grant Balch's last fall; I compare their aftermaths; and I find that in the years between those two mornings, the hunter himself has changed more radically than his country or wildlife. He is now affected, in the woods and on the waters, less by the thrill of anticipation than the seductions of recall.

Another essay might find an analogous change in a man's sexual career. I'll not take up so complex a matter, save to say that the diminishment of either predatory instinct isn't irredeemably grim nor even sad. For it is compensated, one hopes, by an increase in moral judgment.

And by the putting aside of childish things. For it happens that a child had lingered in my spirit far longer than I ever dreamed he would when I was an *actual* child. The mind is its own place, says John Milton's devil, but I seem always late to arrive there; it's only in writing this that I understand where I have come. To watch those birds disappear below Grant's pasture was to watch a boy disappear as well.

It was goodbye, boy. And perhaps good riddance—at least to his storms, bewilderments, agitations. How wouldn't I mourn his death, though, the one with whom I'd traveled so many beautiful miles, and whom I had loved, if ambiguously, for so very long?

Mercy on Beeson's Partridge

IT WAS MY SCREAM, not the knock on the head, that put white spots before my eyes. Nothing lay handy to attack but a metal barrel. I crashed it like a cymbal, spilling rubbish. The racket sent our cat flat-belly across the kitchen floor and downcellar; he'd been watching three chickadees at the window feeder: I half noticed them blow off their perches like seedpods. The dogs hid inside their kennel-houses.

I was, thank God, the only human on hand. But there was more than one of me.

And had always been. Just now I think for instance of a hot afternoon's baseball in my tenth summer, our playing field the back meadow at Sumneytown. I've misremembered my slot in the order, so that when it comes around my teammates all shout, "Syd! Syd!" I linger on the whale-shaped boulder near third, looking for the fellow they're calling. Then someone, not I, walks to home plate. From what seems the sudden height of my seat, I watch him pop lazily to first, then amble over to the rock and climb it to where I perch.

I am on the rock. I.

I—whose age, looks, character, and very gender seem as hazy as the August air.

My motives for connecting that boyish self to the self who decades later would beat up a trashcan may seem equally hazy and ill defined. I appear to inherit from my mother's mother a tendency to oblique association, without her tendency to lay positive emphasis upon it. In any case, pulling that barrel from under our

sink, I rammed my skull against a countertop, and even though
the blow was pretty light—no gash, no blood—my rage so lifted
me that once again I looked down on someone else: a lame man
teetering in my kitchen, waving a cane, searching for something
further to smash. Could he have been the child who so languidly
waved that old bat?

Like anyone, I'd been lamed before, though never seriously
nor for long. The usual run of a young male's sports injuries, little
more. Still I knew certain things, or thought I did: how in health
we forget the body's primacy; how, when bodily health fails, the
spiritual may soon follow; how even then, if we recover in due
course, we simply take up our affairs again, none the wiser. Yet
this time would be different, I was sure. It seemed impossible that
memories of the preceding five weeks would ever dull, that I'd
need to feel an identical wound to resharpen them—or else some
jog as unpredictable, say, as that turn a moment ago to an ancient
inning of ball.

I convinced myself that this time I'd seen into the suffering
and despair the chronically ill must experience. Indeed, my hip
scarcely better after a month than when I first crippled it, I
imagined myself among their ranks. And so there'd be no more of
anything that till now had made me what I was. I might sit in a
blind or on a deer stand, but no more busting the puckerbrush; I
might fish from bank or boat, but no more scrabbling among
slippery rocks in a streambed.

In fancy I'd vainly squeeze two triggers on the thunderous
getaway of a grouse. He lit too far to be chased up again, and thus
in fancy I hobbled from thicket's edge to where I'd parked nearby.
Or I pictured the head-and-tail rise of a trophy brown trout—
there, against the opposite bank, too distant to reach without the
deep wading I couldn't risk anymore. I envied the yellowlegs on
that shore, trotting smartly into the riffle, smartly out, then
strutting like arrogant pimps, bobbing their sound little asses.

At last the great outdoors would have turned dangerous. From
now on, in an April like this I'd pick my way across our paltry
meadow, staff in hand, a sharp eye out for swells and soft spots.
Looking high over the ridge I might see the broadwing hen,
spring's annual genie, and covet her view more than ever. I'd

breathe the mud, the sap, the mist. Then I'd turn for the house in tears.

Come fall, I'd weep too, remembering the scents of a bird cover: frost-slackened apple, cinnamon whiff of dead fern, pungency of the slain grouse itself, pointer's breath in my face as I congratulated her or him on the find. In June I might drive to some old roadside trout haunt: dusk; bats; spinners in their egg-laying dance; slurping fish; the odors of water and weed and gravel. I'd take it all in through my rolled-down window, then start up the new truck, the one without a clutch.

Summer'd annoy and winter scare me. I wouldn't be one of those admirable souls who, squarely acknowledging the goneness of a prior life, start over in a new track. My deepest track was worn through those gamewoods and riverbottoms, and I followed it, even when inobviously, in the craft I had long since chosen. The very notion of another context for my writing spun the brain.

In short, he had vanished, that I I'd known for so many years.

§

I'm supposed to stand six feet, two inches tall, although—bones settling after half a century—I may have shrunk some. At all events, I felt shorter during this period of soreness than I had since eighth grade, when every last girl in town seemed a tower enfleshed. My wife is supposed to stand six feet one, and does, but just then she became one more woman looking down on me, for every good reason, physical and metaphorical: I made a miserable, nasty invalid, whom I myself despised.

I mention my wife in part because of this whole business started with her, whose statuesque height is all in her legs. I, on the other hand, am apelike, nothing but upper torso. While her inseam is a full six inches longer than mine, on taking over the wheel of a car from me, she must tilt the rearview mirror significantly down.

On Robin's thirty-fifth birthday, we contrived to put our preschoolers in the care of a babysitter. For the first time in years, she and I were free to ramble the hills, just the two of us, as we'd done on first marrying. While a good deal of our conversation was of course *about* those children, our outing felt—well, romantic and then some.

Robin herself is March's child, which might in an ordinary late New England winter seem inauspicious. But on this particular day we could halfway imagine all nature smiling in congratulation. The temperature climbed to the middle forties, the sun strong. A snow had fallen overnight, just enough to turn the woods crisp and clean, even as the freshets loosened and sang of springtime. We saw a mink track, a doe who'd made it through the cold months in fine shape, even a precocious warbler, its gilt plumage a shock against the sober hemlocks.

There was a certain steep tote road, about seven years old, near home. Though it meant a detour, we hiked it for the view of Moosilauke. On the way down my wife suddenly stopped and laughed out loud.

"What's so funny?" I asked.

She pointed at our footprints in the snow. I saw, not for the first time, that I needed two strides to cover the distance she made in one. But I laughed back anyhow, because it seemed such a long way from eighth grade, from those idiotic leg-stretching drills I'd invented in the hope of growing tall as my pretty second cousin Anne Longstreth—because here stood my wife, even taller, prettier.

Then Robin broke into a downhill run, catch-me-if-you-can, a willowy woman in a thermal undershirt, a pair of Johnson's green wool pants, a set of felt-lined Sorels, a weathered down jacket cinched around her waist, but—she was that beautiful, she was that desirable—I conjured a fleeing nymph. I took off, for all the world like a bassett on a hare's trail, but I caught and kissed her. She smelled like fresh air.

When she broke again, I tried to match strides with her, laying my feet down in her tracks. Though each pace felt like a broad-jump, I kept at it until I heard an odd little crackling just behind me. Three more strides and I went down like a shot boar.

That strange sound had been the wrenching of hyperextended hip ligaments, but it had taken my brain a moment or two to register the pain, the weakness.

❦

Sound again, I'd recall that pain and that weakness and accompanying moods—mopery of March, fury of April, related miseries of May and June. They'd seem exotic enough by then that I likened my contemplation of them to the sort of research an archaeologist must do. So often and long has he studied, say, the mystic artifacts of the ancient Niger delta that he "knows" them backward and forward; yet they are not his by virtue of that knowledge. Nor will they ever become his unless he can somehow and improbably be drawn into a context where all their originative energies and *felt* meanings operate. He may consciously or unconsciously long for such transport; but he must also sense how awesome, even crushing, it could prove.

I have dug around sufficiently in my period of lameness to have the archaeological knowledge of it, but I can no longer truly feel it from within, even if in certain instants of magical thinking I may want to. Perhaps such a desire passes in my case for intellectual curiosity; a saner self, however, prays that if it should ever revisit the spiritual domain of those months, if it should ever again inhabit the I that I was then, it will do so not in a sickroom—to say nothing of ward or cellblock or nursing home, or any other place that literally shuts a soul in.

❦

The physical end of this story arrived, none too soon, by July, and by August I was back on the track entirely. The mornings and evenings turned brisk, the less hardy trees began to blush, the grouse chicks pushed their adult feathers. I had two veteran gun dogs, but also a green one to work, and at last the time was right for him to meet wild birds.

A mile from my house lay a great beaver flowage, its eastern bank a strip of ground just under a cliff. Narrow as that strip was, its hedges of alder, sumac and berrystalk always held game. The water on one side and the sheer ledge on the other, moreover, were natural checks on a headstrong pup.

That summer the grouse were in cyclical decline, and the Beeson cover—as I called it for its absentee Connecticut owner—harbored only one brood. But this consisted of a half dozen birds, who liked to congregate in a certain northerly corner of the puckerbrush. I could park my truck in Beeson's field, leave the pointer yapping in his crate, walk to the spot, and flush the partridge. Then I could bring my novice back to hunt up the singles, which were mature enough by August that when we arrived the mother hen would simply fly out of the cover, abandoning them temporarily to their own devices. I had other wild thickets in which to train, but this one combined handy terrain with a decent number of grouse, well past being squealers but still adequately naive to stay put while I firmed up a point.

In one case, a spring chick sat *too* well. Before I could get there, my dog broke and grabbed the bird. He killed it, even if he can't have given much of a bite: I dressed and cooked the contraband partridge that evening, but I never found a toothmark. I ate a perfect meal for a single person, my wife and children off visiting her mother at the time.

Perhaps because everything about that meal was illegal—and I couldn't help thinking a bit immoral, despite my innocence—I remember offering a paganish prayer to the hen, penance and gratitude mixed together in it. I'd been walking and even running steadily for several weeks, but the taste of her chick seemed a culminative rite in my healing.

There is a passage in Emerson that I've adored for so long I can all but recite it, and as I lingered at my table, sipping black coffee, missing my family, noting how short the evening shadows were becoming, it crowded my thoughts:

> The writer wonders what the coachman or the hunter values in riding, in horses and dogs. It is not superficial qualities. When you talk with him he holds these at as light a rate as you. His worship is sympathetic; he has no definitions, but he is commanded in nature by the living power which he feels to be there present. No imitation or playing of these things would content him; he loves the earnest of the north wind, or rain, of stone and wood and iron. A

beauty not explicable is dearer than a beauty we can see to the end
of. It is nature the symbol, nature certifying the supernatural, body
overflowed by life which he worships with coarse but sincere rites.

I couldn't speak for the coachman, but I could for the hunter, our
values being identical, and likewise for the writer. Indeed, by the
merest bending of Emerson's observations I could claim that to
write and hunt in the same spirit was to be, as his title implied,
"The Poet" . . . or at least a *sort* of poet.

My sort.

To be that way (the hell with fame and riches) seemed all I
could wish for; and it still does. I recall looking at the backs of my
hands, on which the Beeson brambles had prematurely inscribed a
birdshooter's autumn tatoos. Strange that there'd been no pain in
their making, and certainly none now. In fact, whether because it
was a matter of "body overflowed by life" or not, those red
scratches seemed to feel *good*. Healed, I'd already forgotten the
despondencies of the prior months, forgotten what it was not to
worship—nor be able to worship—nature in sympathy. I was
again the I with whom I'd for so long been most familiar, steeped
in a beauty whose end he could not see.

That I. He was among other things more than ready for his
family to come home. He wanted to touch the good flesh of his
children. He wanted even more to touch the flesh of his marvelous wife, and thus he simply leapt over his interlude of mental
and physical pain to a snowy trail, in fancy watching her glide
downhill ahead of him, virtually defining his notions of the erotic.
This time, of course, he scripted a more appropriate close, in a
wrangled bed.

It was as if he'd never fallen, would never fall again. He could
barely remember the bitter human being who frothed at the
mouth; who stood in his kitchen, dazed, chopping the air with his
cane, ready to raze the whole world.

By further vague association, however, I'll now remember
another person who brandished a cane, her grim lips likewise
flecked with foam. I knew this woman only as Mrs. Greene. She
was a friend of my grandmother's, though everyone in my family
made a great joke of the friendship. For as unfailingly cheerful as

that grandmother remained to the end of her astonishingly active life (she played tennis through her late eighties), so gloomy and angry was Mrs. Greene, although she hung on to her spectacular good looks till the end of *her* long but sedentary life. While my mother's mother was all good-natured non sequitur, Mrs. Greene was all fierce concentration. Indeed, everything about the two women seemed so different that they could scarcely resist—and usually didn't—falling into quarrel whenever they met. My father assumed that they called on one another in order, as he put it, to keep their batteries charged.

There is a certain very large cornsnake that figures prominently in my recall of this Mrs. Greene. One of my younger brothers had found it on a ramble over my uncle's farm and brought it home. By happy coincidence, a younger sister had recently been presented by some thoughtless adult with a pair of white mice. Since these were apparently of opposed sex, their numbers soon multiplied by tens. Before long, of course, my mother was stuck with tending both reptile and rodent, and she conceived the obvious plan: the snake would be fed, and the population of mice controlled.

Now anyone who has ever kept a constrictor knows that its appetite is unpredictable: it may hop right on its prey, or it may lie there for hours and even days, as if unconscious of the prey's existence. Corny, as the snake had been witlessly named, proved more energetic than some, and could generally be counted on to swallow his mouse within a half hour.

Practical-minded as my mother was and is, aware as she was and is of the natural world's sternness, still she felt a tinge of compassion for the mice, who tripped with such moronic fearlessness around Corny's glass cage. Having deposited a rodent, therefore, she would immediately set an egg timer for forty-five minutes. If the creature survived that span, he or she would be lifted out and another put in. My brothers and I called this arrangement Mouse Roulette.

Corny was provisioned well—and perhaps too effortlessly. Indeed, I sometimes surmise it was because he missed the challenge of a stalk that he finally broke from confinement. He did not, however, leave the house: now and then he'd make brief appearances, poking out of a heat register but always ducking back in before someone could nab him.

Enter, from stage left in the living room, Mrs. Greene, for her weekly cup of tea and her fight.

Enter, from stage right, Corny, who stretches more of himself than usual out of the wall-grate, shoots his tongue, weaves like a cobra.

Exit Mrs. Greene, rapidly, for all that she needs a cane. In her rush she scatters the tea service to the floor.

It's still easy, you see, to recall all this as farce, even without the snake. On that bright September afternoon just before Labor Day, I'd made an audience because at twenty-one I was young enough to be amused by an old woman's wrath, and by the hoarse and haphazard chastisement it always earned from another old woman. I never dreamed, though, of anything so comically appropriate as Corny's appearance, a touch that convinced Mrs. Greene that my grandmother—or at least someone from our evil clan—had contrived this whole show.

※

None of us would see Mrs. Greene again for more or less exactly a year, across which I'll hop here. Though by now the evenings had turned clear and cool, the women's reconciliation was to transpire not over tea but over dinner on the back porch—in the open air, where no serpent might be cached.

My parents were up in Maine, fishing. In their absence, I'd been sucking down beer all afternoon with my oldest chum Tommy White. Like most people, I could be much changed by drunkenness. Like most arrested adolescents, I liked to show off. The circumstance, in short, was volatile.

Tommy and I fixed ourselves sandwiches. On a whim I carried mine to the table where the old ladies sat, and he followed me. I gave my grandmother an exaggerated kiss on the cheek, and I greeted Mrs. Greene with a similar, but even more exaggerated one, together with compliments on her appearance, overdone even for so physically beautiful a person as she—who was no fool. She shrugged me off and muttered grimly.

A general silence fell till my grandmother offered a few cheery and diffuse platitudes. The last of the sweetcorn always tasted wonderful. The Phillies had the pennant sewed up at the end of a wonderful season. Lyndon Johnson was a wonderful man after all. It was wonderful too how the Pennsylvania mugginess was fading, and the September breezes starting, and you could just smell the garden's wonderful marigolds—"Naughty Mariettas," she called them, inhaling demonstratively.

"Yes, Bessie," growled Mrs. Greene, "everything is just so damned *wonderful.*"

"Well," my grandmother answered, "better that way than some others."

I winked at my friend—the show was warming up, the batteries charging—but Tommy looked nervous.

"How old are you?" Mrs. Greene suddenly asked, her brilliant, ice-blue eyes seeming to recede into her skull as she studied her friend.

My grandmother, in spite of that fixed stare, justifiably supposed the question addressed to one of us boys. It took her a moment to catch on. "You know exactly how old I am," she finally answered. "Five years older than you are. Why ask such a stupid thing?"

"Stupid?"

"Stupid."

"Well, I was wondering exactly how *you* could live so long and be so stupid."

My grandmother deliberately folded her napkin and set it on the table, a prelude, I was sure, to the dressing down she meant to give her veteran adversary. I beat her to it: "Mrs. Greene," I asked, speaking softly, feigning respectful curiosity, "I was wondering something too."

She turned her gaze my way now, eye sockets become black holes, that glimmer barely discernible within—the frigid light, it suddenly occurred to me, of a snake's stare.

"I wonder why you're such a bitch."

I think back on this crudeness with horror, as if someone else—maybe Tommy—were responsible for it. I'd been irked by this broody woman's assaultive comments to my beloved grandmother, of course, but it was more than a mere rallying to flesh and blood that prompted my own assault. It was liquor, to be sure, but it was somehow hormones as well: for all Mrs. Greene's years, a bizarre, aggressive sexual edge had some part in my treatment of her just then.

All of which, perhaps, is only to say that I ached to be other than my same old well-raised self.

"Yes?" I prodded.

"Yes, what?" Mrs. Greene grunted. But for the eyes her face looked bored, as if she'd encountered—and now I'm sure she had—challenges that put my own dull insult to shame.

"How come—" I began.

"I don't have to answer *you*," she said, her voice drenched in condescension.

"Maybe you can't."

"Oh, I can. Or I could."

"Then you accept the fact that you're a bitch?"

"I accept the fact that you say so, and I accept the fact that you don't know the first thing about anything."

"You can't answer," I said, sensing how foolish and resourceless my taunts appeared, how desperate I was growing—I, who dreamed of becoming an author, a wordsmith.

"I said I don't have to explain."

"You can't."

"The *world* will explain it to you in time, young man. *All* of it."

I turned to my grandmother. She was a woman, God bless her, of whom I simply could not be afraid; but I was curious to see how my oafishness sat with her.

I would not see, for just then I glanced indoors, where my father—stationed so that I alone could detect his presence—beckoned me. I rose without making excuses and went in to him, and to my mother, who lurked even further back in the room.

Both were sun-browned and unkempt.

My father showed the full week's growth of beard.

I noticed that my mother, in a five-and-dime cotton dress, had long hairs on her legs.

They'd sneaked home to deposit their Maine salmon in the freezer and to pick up some clean clothes. They meant to extend their holiday by spending a couple more nights away, in my dead grandparents' cabin out in Montgomery County. I felt mildly hurt to witness their earthy energy, their mischief, their clear lust to be gone again, for in spite of the pleasant anarchy that I and my brothers and sisters always enjoyed under my grandmother's care, I had missed them both. Yet I was relieved as well: in their distraction and hurry, my parents overlooked the fact that I'd been drinking. Moreover, some part of me relished the prospect of further and better outrages toward Mrs. Greene.

By the time I returned to the porch, however, the two old women were onto some other topic of dissension, fairly mild. And I could tell that my friend Tommy, if he'd savored my boorishness in the first place, now wanted to leave as much as my parents had.

"Good night," I said to my grandmother. And then, the devil come back despite me, I made a deep actor's bow to Mrs. Greene. "And good night to you too, Madame Bitter."

"Bitter," she flatly repeated.

"*Madame* Bitter."

My barb seemed no less labored and puny than the others, but Mrs. Greene—wincing with the effort—laid her hands on the glass tabletop and pushed herself to her feet. Next she unhooked her cane from the chairback and raised it overhead. At last I'd made an impression.

"You wouldn't hit me?" I sneered.

"You stand where you are and find out!" she shouted, a runnel of spit flowing down the channel of her frown, that aged face's only groove.

"You'd smash up the whole world if you could," I said.

"I'd love to," she answered. "And you will too one day."

I took a few steps toward her and, her timing faulty, she came up empty as she swung the stick. I stood in my tracks till Tommy dragged me backwards off the porch. Even as I left Mrs. Greene made hatchety gestures in my direction.

※

The autumn after my lameness, the grouse remained as scarce as they'd promised to be during those summer training sessions by

Beeson's beaver swamp. The male dog who'd caught and killed the young bird in August came along nicely, though given more plentiful upland game he'd have come along even better. All through the gun season I needed to return to Beeson's just to make sure he'd get his nose into *something*. Time and restiveness had dispersed the grown chicks to other places, but that faithful hen remained. She was smarter, flightier, harder to pin than the brood she had raised; but she was always there, and she saw my pup into college, as her chicks had seen him through high school.

On the final day of the season, I tramped through miles of woods behind that young dog. All the grouse in New England seemed gone. Dusk descending, I crated my pointer and headed for home. It had been a meager fall, but I remembered enough of the spring preceding to know how much worse it might have been. There'd be other seasons now; those angry and melancholic dreams of myself as an old man with a staff rather than a gun or rod in his hand would not come true for a considerable while.

And yet it was disappointing to think how soon we'd eat our way through the year's harvest of grouse in our freezer: I could feel saliva pool under my tongue at the thought of those few meals. And it was even more disappointing not to have shot a bird over the pup on his last hunt of the autumn, not to have lodged such a kill in his memory for the long coming winter. As I passed Beeson's bog, therefore, I slowed, my mind in conflict. There were some twenty minutes of shootable light remaining in the afternoon, all I needed to locate my hen partridge.

At length I backed up and parked. Breaking the shotgun, I slid one round only into a chamber; I meant to give that grouse all but every advantage. Then I opened the door of the dogbox, slipped the bellcollar over the pointer's head, and followed him toward the brush.

Halfway across the field beside the cover, I kicked a hidden wedge of granite. I must have done so, as they say, just right, for the hip I'd wounded eight months before cried out in pain, and so, falling to the ground, did I—I, who was again in that brief second the self of wan April and not bluff November.

When I got up, my legs were sound beneath me; yet I went on standing for minutes on end, till down in the thicket my dog's bell

quieted: he'd found his bird. Still I stood, waiting for the inevitable fusillade of wings, and afterwards the clank of the moving bell.
As soon as I heard these, I blasted my whistle.

It was time to go home; it was time for mercy on Beeson's
partridge, the constant one, who'd even surrendered a chick to
me and mine.

My eager young pointer was reluctant to come to heel, and I
waited a long spell before he finally did. It was during that spell that
I remembered not merely the bodily pain of a few short weeks
ago, not merely the rage with which I clubbed a wastebasket but
also that last evening with poor, dauntless Mrs. Greene, who
wielded *her* cane like a weapon too.

I recalled the rough beard on my father, who would drop dead
within eighteen months of that night.

I remembered my mother's silky leghairs.

I may even have remembered those pink-eyed mice, and how
blithely they trotted the invisible confines of their glass world
until—at the egg-timer's gong—they were lifted back to a more
familiar realm, or, the gong too late, they were rapt by sudden
coils.

Those coils would unravel, Corny's diamond head be smeared
on the driveway by an unwitting neighbor kid's bike wheels.

My grandmother would fall and break her hipbone and never
be the same woman again, her mind, so often delightfully scattered before, become a permanent and grisly chaos. She would not
recognize her grandchild, me, for her last four years.

Standing in Beeson's field as the light went down, I scarcely
knew that grandchild either. There was once a boy who could not
quite understand his middle-aged parents' romantic silliness; nor
the blackmindedness of his grandmother's quarrelsome companion; nor—as that wondrously handsome old companion claimed
—much of anything at all.

On the Lookout

SURE, you *want* to go hunting. But you can't just up and do
it," I told him. "Not with me or anybody: there's too much
to learn first."

"Like?"

"Guns, getting around in the woods, that sort of thing." I
stopped short of reminding him he'd always been a city kid. As
though that were the major difficulty.

"What if I just *watched?*" he asked.

"Well, maybe . . . ."

"Do you eat what you get?" he growled, steroids having
turned his voice to the hoarse basso that strangers find amusing.

"Of course."

"Can you shoot lambs, Uncle Syd? I *love* lamb."

It's just as well to remember that it had a funny side, my sad
conversation with Tim, three years ago Thanksgiving. He'd already been through his first long siege at a children's hospital in
Denver, where specialists pronounced his case among the worst of
its kind in America.

We'd ended our talk by agreeing to tent overnight on The
Lookout, after summer had slightly lessened his peril. And at last
here we were, on one of those prematurely crisp August afternoons in northern New England. All the haze had been sucked
from the air, and there was a hint of scarlet and gold on the upper
slopes of the White Mountains eastward. Starlings and flickers had
started to congregate, to plan; they exploded from roadside
ditches, fence posts, and powerlines as we drove up route 5. We'd

even seen a small flight of Canada geese high over the Connecticut River, jumpy, getting out early.

My plan was to arrive at height-of-land without climbing too
hard or far to do it. The view would be like nothing Tim had ever
known, and despite the dry month we could safely start a fire on
The Lookout's granite apron. Given my good excuses, I tried to
ignore rubber-burns and crushed witch hazel in the rearview as
we bumped up the ghostly twitch road. When the truck finally
called quits, I unloaded, shouldered the whole of our gear except
for the boy's pack—a faded yellow-and-green affair with a snarl-
ing cougar on its flat, nothing but muscle and maw. Yet the thing
was tiny and underloaded enough to fit to a doll.

We'd pause now and then in the short climb while Tim regathered breath; his pose during those lulls seemed almost willfully dramatic, backlit as he was, the piney ridge to west dark
behind him. If I hadn't known the child, looking down that slope
I might have imagined precocious physical strength, and not just
spiritual: his chest had swelled bearlike in nine years of struggling
for air.

It took us a good spell to reach our granite slab. New to all this,
uncertain and nervous, I let another go by before lifting the
portable inhalator from my Adirondack basket. Leveled on the
rock amid browned hemlock needles, rodent-fretted acorns and
deer droppings, the machine—all plastic gauges, vents, and knobs
—seemed otherworldly. I started at it for several moments, one
palm laid on its housing, as if it might suddenly burst into flight.
Fumbling with my other hand, at last I found the list prepared by
his mother, my wife's sister. I scanned it, then let go of the
machine and stood two vials on the stone.

"Not *those*," Tim whined, scooping and flinging them back
into the basket. "Those are *morning* meds."

"You sure?" I mumbled.

"Look at the *paper.*" Like most kids his age, he can speak in
italics. Rereading the instructions, I found him right, and I shivered some. Good thing one of us had kept on the ball.

Having no choice, we fell quiet while the machine hissed. I
watched Tim's brown eyes, lively above the mask, playing across
the vista all the way to Mount Moosilauke: its southwest flank's

glacial-erratic tumbles, the gray-green lichen spread on its higher promontories, cloud-shadows racing up and over, the mountain at large a testimony both to permanence and mutability—strong medicine, as the vanished Ordanaki might have said.

From our perch we also saw a gorgeous oxbow in the Connecticut, two miles down, where a flock of snow geese had loitered all summer. I could just make out their broad, pale smear on water and mudbar. Even from this distance, since May I'd been hearing the birds' dog-yappy palaver. No question of that now, of course—not with the inhalator's ruckus and Tim's loud gulps. The unrightness of things seemed almost palpable.

Yet I felt easier than I'd expected after all these months of anxiety. The boy's condition, in and of itself, had worried me less through winter and spring than the fact that it so rarely freed him, even for mild adventure. What if he found this one a bore? What if he began dreaming out loud—as I'd frequently heard him do—of Disney World, of shaking hands with Mickey and Goofy, all the synthetic creatures? The glint in Tim's big eyes instantly calmed such fears: he was gratified, maybe even excited.

I checked my watch and got up on my feet, kicking a petty avalanche of oak nuts down the sidehill. "Mast for my big buck," I silently said, recalling the great hindquarters bunching for his jump across this very ridge-crest, out of my sights before I could fire. Night coming on, I'd cursed the end of a season in which I daily, futilely took that noble track. But I'd blessed it too.

There were ten minutes left in Tim's treatment. I meant to site the tent while we waited them out, but before I could move, the boy tugged at my pantsleg. When I looked into them, the eyes were filled with something new—fear? anger? impatience? disillusionment? Nothing good anyhow. I sat back on the ledge, imagining the archaic .30 Remington across my knees, the jewel-like coruscations of frost and mica in the ledge, the tang of November air. I tasted that strange, coppery taste far back in my throat, the way I had when I heard the big whitetail grunt upwind on opening morning.

At my signal, Tim clicked the shutdown button, then carelessly yanked away the mask. We could talk again. "What was the matter?" I began. "Were you worried—"

"I feel a lot better now," he broke in. And then, like every child on earth, he asked, "What's there to *do?*"

"Well, suppose I get our camp rigged and you find us a little wood?"

He grinned, turned, went up the slab and over. Not like a deer. The Boston Bruins logo of his jacket hung momentarily behind, odd afterimage.

It's never easy to locate a piece of ground flat and broad enough for a tent on The Lookout. When I found one, I went down on hands and knees, probing an anthill to see if it was active. It wasn't, so I cuffed away sticks and cones to smoothe our beds. Then I joined tentpoles, set aside U-stakes, hitched support lines to tree trunks fore and aft.

Such fiddling always moves me to reverie. I noticed the square knot in my fly-cord and in the instant recalled when and where I'd tied it—fifteen years ago; Finnegan Point; Fourth Lake; a dawn broken into sun after a nightlong downpour. My friend Don Metz and I used up the daylight hiking to the summit of Washington Bald and back. By the time we reached camp again, bone-weary, famished, blissful, the hemp had shrunk and popped between two hemlocks. I shook my head, and not only over remembered folly. Even a decade and a half ago, what kind of man would pack so old-fashioned a tent, heavy canvas, hempen guys and all? But here I was, packing it still, an heirloom from my father.

I whacked the last peg in with the flat of my axe, and straightened. How much time had scurried by now, on The Lookout? Suddenly my brain crowded with grim fantasies, and I scooted off to search for Tim. But soon enough I found him, languidly tugging at a yellow birch, bigger around than he was, standing dead.

"No," I said, my admonishment more like a sigh. "Just snap off these underbranches"—I cracked a skinny pine limb, punk puffing in the breeze like milkweed—"and bring me a bunch." He stood, as if confounded. I added, "All we need is a cookfire, okay?"

"Okay," he whispered, shooting me a look, half embarrassed, half pouty.

"Still a couple things to do," I said over my shoulder, heading down the ledge again, resolved to give him another few moments alone.

Once I'd spread the cook-kit, I picked out my dinted frypan and threaded on the handle. Then, fitting my pot's bale into its holes as I went, I made for a springhole I knew. There was a coolness over the water when I got there, a few translucent midges dancing through it. With one hand I skimmed some spent insects and pinespills from the surface, dipping gently with the other, not to rile things up. I retreated a single step, but suddenly stopped to drink the old pot dry in a long swallow. Soot and tin and cold: tastes like haunts, to keep a fellow wakeful at night, his memories bearing down.

I knelt again, refilled in a hurry, and quick-walked back to the fireplace. Then I stepped up the apron for another peek at Tim. he was bent at the waist, as if to study the pile of sticks he'd gotten together in my absence. Or rather the small layer: five, maybe six.

"Not going to hold us," I said. "Burns fast. Softwood."

"Soft?"

"Trees with needles. Softwood. It burns fast." I repeated.

"Didn't seem soft to *me*."

Lord, had this little played him out? "You tired?"

Still bent, he dismissed the question with a curt wave. "Nah."

"Then get cracking, pal." I gave him a slightly forced, comradely grin. "Your uncle cooks bad after dark."

Tim's case is more than asthma, and is so excruciatingly complicated that doctors give it a simple name, as if —I've imagined —they could thereby reduce it to something manageable. They call it Failure to Thrive. In Tim's instance that means a rock and a hard place: his drugs let him breathe, at the same time turning his bones nearly to powder and playing hell with his immune system. If that's not worry enough, according to the physicians they will also produce emotional damages in time. Perhaps they already have. The matter's cloudy.

I know all this. I knew it then. Yet the boy's sloth and aimlessness began to irritate me. Hell, I thought, he's no different from any other nine-year-old, hot for the fun and cool to the work. I watched him blunder around for five more minutes, random as a sleepwalker, and then I barked, "*Get moving!*"

Of course I hadn't blinked before calling myself a heartless bastard. But I tried to rationalize as well: Wouldn't it be worse to hide how I was feeling? Wasn't it better to treat Tim, precisely, like any nine-year-old?

Oh, sure.

I went back to the cooksite, and he slouched after me a few minutes later, clutching his firewood in his small hands like a nosegay. By then I'd already scraped up some wood of my own, and anyway Tim was due for another bout with the inhalator. His mother had suggested that under these unusual circumstances we shorten the intervals between doses of Ventolin, but slightly cut the doses too, one measure of safety as usual begetting its complementary risk.

I got the system running. Tim wouldn't meet my eye, and this time when I got up he never moved. I sneaked over to the tent and, crawling inside, unpacked my tiny radio. Needless to say, I felt guilty. It wasn't merely that I'd left my nephew hooked up behind me, stewing in his own juice, nor that I was keeping my radio a secret. It was also that I had a radio in the woods to begin with: some worlds shouldn't mix. Yet I'd justified such a violation earlier in the day, when I nestled the inhalator into my basket. If we were going to have electronics at The Lookout anyhow, why not listen to the Red Sox after the boy fell asleep? The game would be out in Milwaukee; it would be 8:30 before the first pitch, a late enough bedtime even for a healthy child.

I held the radio against my off hip and came out of the tent. Stepping a few yards into the scrub, I hid the thing, then made a big show of zipping my fly as I ambled back to our ledge. Short of the firesite I stopped to spy from behind some greengrowth, and saw that my slyness was wasted. Tim had apparently forgotten my very existence; he scanned the valley again, same as before, except that above the mask his face seemed robbed of animation. He suddenly reminded me of a Vedic contemplative, completely still, spine straight, spidery legs folded under him. I could imagine it wasn't the inhalator's hiss that cut him off from the early evening's quick, abundant noises: red squirrels scampering through dry leaves, a thrush's gong, the grating of a loner raven, a doe or fawn bleating over in the burntland. I could almost believe that some nonspecific sound in Tim's *mind* had voided all these, and much else, had brought that blankness to his countenance, a blankness just perceptibly crossed by disenchantment.

Once the treatment was over, though, I attributed such gloomy vision to the visionary: me, too often inclined to morose interpretation. Tim himself seemed reinvigorated, mostly by hunger.

"I could eat a whole cow!" he shouted, wrecking my silly figure of the Hindu mystic.

"You're hungrier in the woods."

"*I'll* say I am!"

"And food tastes better too. You'll see."

"*When?*"

"Twenty minutes, twenty-five?"

Tim wriggled, humped his shoulders. Remembering the first thing he'd un packed on arrival, I thought of a way to help kill his wait. He was visibly proud of the knife—never mind its chips, its rust-stains, its feckless edge—so I showed him how to cut shavings along our kindling, just as I'd shown my own oldest boy, just as I'd show my younger children when their turns came. Just as my father had shown me. But had I labored like Tim, had my tongue sprawled out of my mouth, had the job gone as slowly? Yes, yes, and yes, I was certain. Teaching this trick to my son, though, had I hidden my impatience as well as my father must have done? Did I adequately hide it now? Those answers were less clear.

We stacked the wood, shaved sticks on the bottom. Tim lit a match and raptly watched the curls flame up like paper. I sighed, rapt too, the fire catching hold for fair. I've always understood the appeal of pyromania at least halfway—a longing for exquisite conflagration, racing through the rainbow to whiteness, to purity.

I set the pan on, and after a few minutes laid four strips of bacon inside.

"Bacon?" Tim asked, his heavy brows arching.

"Need it for frying."

"My dad wouldn't let me eat bacon, Too greasy."

Of course he wouldn't want anything *bad* for you, I thought. That's why he lit out—couldn't stand the pain. Noticing the blanch of my knuckles as I jostled the pan, I checked myself: "Oh, a little grease won't harm you out here." Tim's smile was only a flutter, but I caught it and winked.

The hot fat spat and steamed, its odor melding with those of warm granite and my own sweat and the evergreen needles above and beside and around us. It mixed as well with the countless stored sensations of youthful, backcountry campouts: a chew of spruce pitch on Ball Ridge; the miraculous weight in my hand of that chain pickerel I'd caught from Junior Stream when I was seven; the scent of coal oil in Carter White's lantern at Fourth Lake; Uncle George MacArthur, whiskey-singing "The Shores of Gaspereau" on Third; a small feed of yellowlegs, poached out of season in the heath behind Gull Island, and—as we sat on the rocky beach that evening—ancient Earl Bonness, a stream of the birds' savory juices spilling from his outlaw grin. I began to feel a little charge of juice under my own tongue. There was one in my eyes, too. From the smoke.

After the bacon stiffened to brown, I drained it, ranging the four strips side-by-side on a paper sack, orderly. They seemed downright pretty like that, but I told Tim to help himself. Deliberately begging the loan of his sorry knife, I chunked potatoes into the pan, worrying them back and forth till they also were done—glistening, golden. Then I scraped them into another sack and propped it beside the fire to keep warm. When I looked back at the child, his eyes were closed. What did he see inside? He was eating the bacon, very slowly. All of it.

At that Thanksgiving reunion, Tim had told me he *loved* lamb, and I owed him a feed of it on the strength of the verb alone. Driving to The Lookout I'd stopped at Wings' market to buy five chops. They looked pretty too, red and dense on the bone-white wrapping paper, one of whose corners I tore off to clean what smut I could from my camp grill's spokes. I flipped the scrap into our fire. The grease spots darkened, then exploded. Blue to yellow to orange. I propped the grill, slid a couple more sticks under it, and eased the lamb cuts on top.

The sun flared and set as we feasted on the potatoes and broiled meat, Tim wolfing his own three chops and half my second one. I stayed a bit hungry, even after we'd devoured a pair of sugar-shiny store donuts apiece, but although a little too much pathos hovered on that twilight scene to say I felt happy, I did consider myself at least successful.

By the time the full moon's dome began to show over Moosilauke, Tim was half-asleep. I spoke to rouse him, early moonlight being always the best of it: "Toss your bones way out over the ledge."

"Isn't that litter?" he mumbled.

"Not for the animals."

"Huh?'

"Just throw them far enough the skunks won't visit. Give them to the coons and coyotes and bears."

He sat up at that. "There's bears here?"

"Sure."

"But—"

"But they'd sooner run clear down to your house than get near a person."

"You positive?"

"Positive."

Now Tim became a whirl against the moon's face, flinging his leavings toward the valley. I could hear them break the canopy, well below us. Not a bad arm, in spite of everything.

When he came back to the fire, a little breathless, he sat closer to me than before. As the moon climbed, it gradually erased the westerly shadow of Moosilauke, which had stretched all the way to the river beneath us. The marsh on the New Hampshire side suddenly lightened, and some night fowl flushed in our direction; I leaned forward, curious, but the bird quickly found another shade and disappeared inside it, headed who-knows-where.

Once the moonball floated entirely clear of the ridge, I saw it wore a wet halo. Rain coming, I supposed, but probably not before we could break camp in the morning. Pilasters of mist filed northward, at last crowding together over the marshy setback from which the bird had flown. In the main river, I could just see my father and Uncle George in their E. M. White canoe, George half-crouched in the stern, poling southerly along the New Hampshire bank. But then they disappeared into that deeper fog by the marsh, and I felt a little pang: those were men who'd always protected me in life.

Someone else was lining a canoe the other way, upstream across the flats on the Vermont side. Despite the boggy footing, he lifted on his toes as he walked, so I knew it was Don. Maybe he had come to find me where I sat—not hunting for ducks, which weren't in season yet, just scouting in a good place—a hundred yards above him. Maybe he meant to tell me hello. Maybe my brother Jake would show up too, or one of my longtime grouse partners: Landy Bartlett; Joey Olsen; Terry Lawson.

The air over my blind was swarming with black duck and teal. I watched them pour through the next yoke north of The Lookout: singles, little threads, full flocks. I could hear their gabble, the pop and music of their wings. When I looked at the water again, Don wasn't anywhere to be seen; no one was. I must have dozed a while after that, because the moon had risen several degrees by the time my retriever finally woke me, leaning heavily on my left thigh.

It wasn't my dog at all, of course. It was Tim, slumbering in my lap. I leaned to hear him breathe: so *that* was the whistle and clap I'd taken in dream for duckflight. I improvised an ungainly prayer for all the people I'd loved and been loved by. For humanity in general. For animals as well—all the world's fragile flesh.

Suddenly Tim's breath loudened. I started, half-waking him. But wrong again: it was only the late freight from St. Johnsbury, hooting up near Barnet or McIndoe Falls. I checked my watch— already after nine. The Sox would have batted once against the Brewers by now. It was time for Tim's last treatment. His face looked achingly innocent, the skin pellucid with moon, as I drew the plastic mask over his nose. I inserted the medicine cup and flipped the switch; the boy began to breathe still harder, by habit, even in sleep.

There were several fine reasons just then to hate his contraption, its whoosh all the noiser for the night's calm: I could detest it simply for being necessary; for traducing the wildness around us; for its mere *look*, the plastic shell transforming soft moonbeams to a single ugly glare. I could take my pick.

When time was up, I stood Tim and helped him stagger to our tent, wrapping my arms around the barrel chest—lightly, fearful of the ribs' brittleness. A man should carry a boy that drunken with drowsiness, but I didn't dare. I unzipped the mosquito veil and worked him into his bag. It was too late in the season and too cool to worry about bugs, so I left the netting open and lingered to make sure he was really out. Soon his breath settled back into steady rhythm, however full of rustles and hinge-squeaks, and I padded off to the hiding place.

Having peed for real this time, I carried my radio to the fire. Poking up coals to heat the last of my coffee, I tuned in. The Sox were already down by three, so I shut the game off, in the instant hearing the moan of the St. J. freight again, as close as Wells River by now. I wondered that I could treasure the sounds of a train in the woods, while less than a minute of radio babble and static had made me uneasy, not to mention the noise of Tim's damnable inhalator. Whatever my reasons, on The Lookout I felt a romance in that mournful whistle, could all but *see* its notes snaking over the knolls and through the low passes, coming my way from north, slow almost as the antique locomotive herself, as much a physical, man-made force, but benign.

A barred owl, hearing too, began his eight-note chant, which was answered by another somewhere below me toward the river, and then by a couple of coyotes over on the New Hampshire side. My entire reach of valley seemed full of magic alto, cut by animal descant and birdy decrescendo.

The strong coffee tasted better than it probably was.

Tim was lost to this world, and I was sorry. Or at least I guessed so. If he'd heard all that mix of song, he might—out of one feeling or another—stay awake like me, which surely wouldn't be good for him. Ever. When you're failing to thrive, you must need a lot of rest just to stay even. On the other hand, how rare it is for any of our lives to open onto a domain like the one I could see and hear from The Lookout. The fog was climbing the palisade under me more quickly than I'd expected: lovely, haunted, shot with bizarre lights. Within the moon's aureole, some planet opened and closed its eye. Moosilauke seemed to fuse with the sky, or the other way around, mountain extending forever heavenward, heavens come all the long way down to ground.

The night was so marvelously liquid I felt I might float on it. But I started to fret about rain again, about Tim getting wet in the tent. The ledge would puddle up quickly. I resolved that if it came to that, I'd move him out in the dark, return another time to clear camp. The gear would be safe; I'd seldom seen another human being on The Lookout.

The thought settled me. Never a human, except for me, my few hunter chums, beloved members of my family. That seemed supremely fine. Good riddance, too, to human machinery—to my own truck, parked out of mind downhill, to the radio I wouldn't click on again, to my household furnace, oven, water-pump, lamps.

And the machine that kept Tim alive?

Whenever I arrive at it, this is a hard kind of turn, child as I inevitably am of progress, but homesick too for an age that in fact I never knew. What age would that be anyhow? Maybe one in which, if you didn't come into God's country on foot, you came at least by train. But of course that meant you died, you went backwards if you took certain sorts of sick, no matter how young or old you were. You failed to thrive. There was testimony to that in the deepest of these Yankee woods—pitiable headstones, eroded inscriptions. What kind of trade-off would I make, what risks accept? What would I want to do even now, if those were my own lungs over there, within a tent, full of fog and labored song?

Sometimes an answer will come too easily, resolution simply *offering* itself, like grace. And right enough, just then someone came burning up the waterlot road in a car too hot by half. I winced to hear the engine's snarl, the tires chirping with each shift, the caterwaul of hard rock blasting through open windows. The driver was probably some native son of the region: some redneck kid, probably pleased as hell that—unlike his father and his father's father—he'd never spread manure on skinflint pasture nor pull rocks from it; probably lustful to bursting for the girl beside him, near as air; probably smelling that thunderstorm smell in his nose after the six or eight beers they'd shared, a scent you can only pick up before you're all the way grown.

The boy was young, tough, happy. He'd never die . . . and to hell with him.

I sat a long while after, waiting for something. It turned out to be the eight-noter and his comrade, hailing each other again along the sidehill. Then the coyotes started up too, and I could feel my teeth unclench, a chill on them as I grinned into the night.

"To hell with the humans," I said.

Something in me didn't want to say that, but I said it anyhow, right out loud, this being more like it, this being how God planned it, Tim asleep and his loud machine shut down, the rackety hotrod passed into silence, and even the train. When the country is so, you can enter it properly, think the things you should, hear the sounds you're meant to hear. To hell with every bumbling woman and man; the land has its claims too. And the beasts and the birds and the reptiles and bugs. And the quiet that is never a quiet. Chitter of rodents in the dampened moonlight. Bittern's thump down in the marsh. Owls, coyotes corresponding. Acorns and pinecones dropping to earth and ledge—little pops, little papery crashes.

It never lasts, that mood, that sense of conclusion. Not if I stay awake. From the tent there came the harsh clap of a cough, imploding. Right then I'd been thinking there was nothing on earth more important than what I could gather of earth's own being with my senses. But I was on The Lookout because other folks weren't. I'm always up there, or up or out elsewhere, for the same reason, and other folks need to *stay* gone, if I'm to have what I have.

That night there were campers, too, in the middle of Manhattan, Boston, Buffalo, Chicago, even White River Junction . . . but they'd still be camping when the snow flew. Come the end of summer vacation, there'd be a kid somewhere, city or country, staying up as late as this, chewing on the stub of her pencil, the door to her minuscule room shut against her mother and her mother's unpredictable manfriend. The girl would be trying to sort figures in a math book, because—never mind how they teased her on the playground—she's always been determined by God to rise up or die trying; the little bear on her desk wears a white college sweatshirt. And back to my west, in meadowland reverted to prime cover for grouse and hare, how many wall-building, sore-spined, gut-empty sodbusters had given the lie to the Good Old Days?

The hell with the humans, I'd said.

Not ten yards away, Tim's clouded lungs resumed their keening, but stayed loud enough to be heard above the wildsong that had held me. The fog touched my soles now. Firelight came through it, and moonlight, bathing my boots and the woods and the hill and the granite in an eerie phosphorescence. Like x-ray.

I'd looked out on a valley and I'd listened to precious sounds and I'd decided there was nothing important as this. But of course there was, there is.

II

Waiting for the Fall

The Dream of Sickness: Letter to LB in Vermont

To whom do I turn
for understanding if not to you
who with me turned from the gun dog locked on point;
from the big trout's dimpling rise
from the chop of a hound, down in a chilly greengrove,

to look back over the land we had connected
to be here now,
where meaning seemed to be?
To whom if not to you?
I have traveled here to Ontario. It's August.

At home, the air
has stood on end for weeks
full of exhaust, the mountains milky,
the condominiums sprouting like steeple bush.
Whom do I know there? What *is* "there"?

Here, already, loons are bunching.
A clean wind cuffs both bay and bigger water,
white waves everywhere.
A month ahead of us,
the weather

puts me in mind of you, of us, of woods—
the asters at the edge of cover
freezing brown from blue; the last bees' hums;
the rodents gorging berries just before
they're sundered from the stalk—

dark smears on mulch and trail.
When I say *we*, that's what I see,
you know. And all I haven't time to list,
as if a catalogue would do:
the long hikes home, bone-weary,

feather, scale, skin, blood
annealed to one another and you and me;
conversant love for all that got away,
for where it was (wherever): for the promise
of other days in which our hearts

might read, according to old habit,
slue and stream and draw and sidehill—
those places rich with possible surprise,
though it wasn't after all our years surprise
so much as something that held its charge

and graced our dedication.
We watch those places die.
And even all this way above Toronto,
above the lesions of miserable railside shanties,
above the perishing farms

and the second growth of spindled softwood—
even here (this *up* that for so long
has been our dream of last resort),
the power launches snarl their disregard
of our old friend and hex the wind,

and white pines show the shiny scars
that trail bikes skin.
Landy: so much to talk about
and nothing.
Like everyone,

I guess I've looked
for all these years for what's called recreation,
even as heart and mind go sick,
since what is left to us
whereby we might create again

all that held us there
where thirty years ago one heard at dusk

the whirr of farm machines
and the quizzy calls of evening birds alone?
All that held us together?

Even after dark last night
the wind persisted. I lay in a cabin
long hours,
inhaled the jab of air with the pine upon it,
took in the wail of loons that mourned for fish,

imagined myself—all terror-driven—
coursing against my will
to that gaggle of glaring lights on a further shore,
among which tape cassettes blared out
a dozen songs at once,

each like the other,
steady electric backbeat basses
shivering boughs, the understory empty
now of pelt and feather and breath.
I in a papery slip of canoe.

In the dream that came at last, your death was coming.
Yet I thought it mine as well,
for I found myself unable
to utter a single sound as there you lay
and something closed on our camp.

We is a compact.
We, the name of that frail cabin.
We, an organism
composed of softwood needle, alder bush,
aspen stem that surrenders the leaf in storm,

the leaf that falls, the others that fell
to the triumph of autumn
that we might see
—if only in that culminating moment—
the cagey grouse or buck or snowshoe hare

as it crossed a forest alley.
We, a mode of reading.
In the pure clear rain.
In the apple-tartened breeze
that is partly pain, part of the composition.

Against such reading the written word
seems nothing—either a shot or cast that misses
or kills the prey for good,
the prey that will not rise again
as ours did all those seasons,

the single bird, beast, fish an avatar,
the next a recreation,
and the next and next and next and next and next . . . .
You lay there, single body, mute with illness.
Nor could I speak, nor could I make connection.

Your hair, uncanny blond into your fifties,
is uncannily the shade, exact,
of fall-kissed marsh grass on an ancient morning
when the black ducks chuckled,
looked our decoys over, came.

Your skin's the tawn of that hill just as the sun
presented itself again
after we'd joked and recollected,
huddled beneath a generous spruce
those hours out of storm;

or is the flank-shade of a trout
which has long lived in clean sand.
And you were dying.
To whom if not to you will I turn for understanding?
You were dying.

And everywhere
the whirl and clack

of some army coming.
Your heart and mind are turf and stone
and fur and freshet and down,

yet in a dream
they ticked like tires over asphalt seams,
rushing to and from
some wretched city.
Ticked toward death.

Awake, what solace?
I felt for the phone,
but what was left to do?
Repeat our litany
of ready interpretation,

how much of this seems personal attack:
backhoes draining the marshes, their rootings
as if some evil demon yanked our hair;
the scar of Jeep and trail bike on a limb
as if our skin were peeled and burning.

The slick-tongued deejay in the dancing club
maintains his chatter
over the tink and chunk
of ice in high-priced tumblers,
while our hearts and minds detect a demon,

and not that *genius loci*
who was a whiff of presence
above our *we*—that you-and-me
and dog   game   rain
gun   fish   sun.

What else to do except protest
that love is not enough,
our spirits so bound up in things
we cannot here or there or ever
make again?

Or must we just attend
the buzz of tension wires beneath our words
that race along the lanes
—all highways now, all crowded
with hurtling chrome and steel—

before we're disconnected?

Summer

S EASON OF ENDLESS afternoons and vast school vacations,
it recalls the careless days of childhood. If you can dream
yourself back to ten years old, then the time stretching from
now till your next birthday represents a full eleventh of your life,
and the summer more than a quarter of *that* big lazy chunk.
When the warm months arrive we remember a Golden Age.

All this is a commonplace. It's also a sentimentality, at least for
me, who even at ten detested July and August, and particularly
their uninterrupted, mid-Atlantic mugginess. I live now where
the summer's less oppresive, but let it contain a single day of
above-average heat and I'm reminded of a boy's liquid nights in
Pennsylvania, when he'd rise to soak a bath towel; lying under it,
he'd feel his intimate sweat pool instantly with the water. Downstairs the grownups—mother, father, grandmother, resident uncle —ceaselessly murmured to one another, the drone of their
undifferentiable remarks blending with the dull clamor outside of
evening bugs, and the whole wash of listless sound providing an
appropriate link between today's inanition and tomorrow's.

Grown into my teens, I would suffer related miseries. I can still
feel a prickliness like the Nessus shirt, chaff spilling from mammoth haybales as I struggle to load another uncle's flatwagon.
"You ought to been born tall 'stead of fat," says a mean, cackling
hired man at every cutting. The stuff anneals itself even to the
parched membranes of mouth and nose, its branny savor mixing
with the miasma of dust and diesel.

Tall 'stead of fat. In memory that laborer, Red, repeats his insult, over and over, to thickening laughter. And there is nothing for it: his freckle-spattered arms are big around as bales themselves. He has spent a stretch of time in prison, I've heard, for strangling his wife's black lover. I believe that tale, if only for the crude tattoo he wears just under a shoulder. I've seen its style on other scary characters: the ink a peculiar blue, hard to distinguish from the blood-hue in Red's raised veins, the orthography like that of a desperate, hasty note. The writing wavers, as a child's may before some schoolmarm or -master convinces that child to "stay on the line." The tattoo's message is both incomprehensible and frightening: BLESS MY SOUL OR DIE HARD.

Deerflies.

Locust-chant.

Trees at field's edge so dense and droopy with leaves I can't see five yards into the woods.

❧

The high summers of my childhood seemed, in short, all dank infusion and severed connection at once, what a person must sense as he drowns, cut off from his native, quickening air. For me it is at best a period of waiting for autumn—and continues to be.

True enough, I've often treasured June, at least back when the mayflies would hatch throughout a day. But that good month has changed, all but leaving me behind. I don't praise it in myself (just the opposite), but after four decades on the water I've pretty much failed to retain the mere joy of Being There. Nor have I the wit to transcend my disenchantment by relativizing the game, by making an eight-incher among five-inchers look like a prize. I wish I could.

It's said that one ages into patience, but I often worry that I've done the opposite, at least so far as a fish is concerned.

"You know our trouble?" Landy Bartlett once asked me.

We were sitting on a lovely and familiar Vermont streambank, not casting. Mindful of the canny native browns that used to feed in that stretch, we were damned if we'd try those puny, recklessly slurping, put-and-take rainbows. My friend's question was of course rhetorical, but, given our longstanding affection, I played along.

"No," I lied. "What *is* our trouble?"

"We had it too good when we were young."

Be that as it may, I do find myself unwilling anymore to work for a trout unless the fish be larger and harder to fool than such free-risers as I'm lately apt to meet in nearby rivers. Yet I'm uninterested in other species.

How account for this unhealthy rigidity of mine? Some will immediately whiff snobbery in it, but they'll be wrong. If I decline an invitation to a bass outing, say, it's not the patrician angler's contempt for that doughty fish that stops me but the uncertainty that such a trip, no matter how successful otherwise, won't answer a curious longing.

Once I pursued the bass with enthusiasm, but to do so now, while it inevitably links me to my boyhood, falls short of providing other, more mysterious connections, ones I'm groping for even as I write this down, ones that I suppose must be spiritual more than historical. Perhaps that very distinction is foolish, since the timeless must—this side of the grave—be manifest in time. But if while fishing I'm ever to find these connections, whatever they be, I'll need cold water and a trout.

And I'll need to *see* what I'm casting to, partly, I suspect, because I've always been eager to graft hunting impulses onto angling. In any case, I'm seldom inclined (at least in the east; out west's another matter) to beat a river with subsurface streamer of nymph.

If I've got a prayer, given all my stipulations, of doing things the way I like after the cool goes out of the air and the waters settle into their summery torpor, it'll be during the last few minutes of true evening—or more likely even later. I'll pull my hatbrim down to block the last of the daylight's glare or the first of the moon's, then position myself in the streambed just so, searching the little dimple that indicates a late feeder. I will guess at the cast and drift of my invisible fly.

The best trout I've ever taken in New England have come to me at such times, and that's one part of why I adore fishing at night; but the other and greater part is this: some of my most tenacious thoughts have arrived then too.

Yet even night-fishing seems a less and less rewarding technique on either count as our local rivers turn vinegary with poison rain. The insect hatches are rarer and rarer, and, when they do occur, the rises fewer and fewer—and more dispiriting. They aren't the booming resonances of precious memory but the busy, splashful frenzy of small, unselective fish—"sandwich-sizers," as Landy and I call them, though neither of us has kept a trout to eat in a decade or more.

So there I sit, morose and angry at once, muttering about the effects of pH on aquatic entomology, a subject I frankly understand less well than I should, but one not meant anyhow for some story I ache to tell. The terms are too different.

Or I simply stay home, fantasizing about the annual western trip I'll take after Labor Day with Landy and my brother Jake— the broad, cold currents, the wide-girthed wild fish, the air so dry and crisp and chill that coyote and hawk cries seem to fade the minute they are uttered.

But such fantasy itself is undercut by pathos. A theme of my indefinite narrative, after all, is this: a fellow shouldn't be obliged to roam. And true enough, I'd once have regarded fishing elsewhere than on some gorgeous local flowage as a mark of insanity. But then again, a fellow shouldn't be obliged either to linger in home territory through July and August. Just waiting. For nothing.

❦

Of course I've greatly exaggerated. I do have things—not to mention people, above all my family—to engage the mind and soul throughout these months I complain of. Although as Cheever said it's like cheering the Trojans, I root on the Red Sox with more passion than becomes a person of middling age and education. If no words flow down my arms to the keyboard, I can go out and row those arms into delicious fatigue on the beautiful Connecticut River, one mode of exhaustion replacing an inferior other. The children are out of school as well, and there's many a project to dream up with each.

With the passage of years, moreover, I'm keener and keener to how soon a coolness will arrive, a cycle come round; there's no need of my hurrying autumn anymore by persistently longing for it.

The wait for fall is *not* nothing. Not quite yet, despite the fact that our land and its game now face the very attacks that have debased our water and its fish.

I can still perk up, observing the grouse broods' progress. The chicks explode like bumblebees, and the hen trails a wing to decoy me elsewhere.

Their numbers so fallen with the wreck of their habitat, and their escape so slow compared to grouse-flight, I can't bring myself to shoot woodcock anymore; I use them instead to train puppies or to refresh my veteran pointers. And yet my blood still pumps when I see the summer spirals of native birds and hear their wingsong; a time of life comes back to consciousness—a time when blood quickened in anticipation of a flush, a shot, a retrieve, a doe-eyed little bird in my hand. First inklings.

As early as the third week of July, I can detect in sapling and sucker the gemmy hue that will be general in the best season, when I'll be trimming the bodily flab taken on in months preceding, and again, the spiritual.

Spiritual flab? Exactly so, at least for one inclined to read his soul in terms of natural context, one who has habitually considered summer the season of clutter and surfeit: sidehills that I'll hike in boots or snowshoes are thick as ocean during the hot months; the nemesis deerflies of childhood return, in all their whining ubiquity, though these days it's the bald top of my head that draws them; blackflies swarm as well, and mosquitoes, whose annual invasion one tends to forget over a long winter.

And spiders. I've read that there are a million per country acre, and although I haven't a thing against them—admirable hunter/anglers themselves—their legions seem to string snares between every pair of trees in the summer forest. I come out of those woods festooned, frame and mind equally befuzzed. I yearn for clarity till I almost scream.

Clarity. Yes, that's what I'm after, even if I betray my woeful quaintness by saying so.

When not involved in domestic matters, I hunt (more than I fish) and I write, pursuits increasingly regarded either with indifference or, to put it gently, suspicion. As a practitioner of "literature," I've long since accepted the extinction of what Virginia

Woolf called The Common Reader in an age of mass media. Such audience as I'll ever command will be eccentric and small, but I can live with that, almost preferring it. As a practitioner of a blood sport, I resigned myself some while ago to living not so much with indifference as hostility from certain quarters, including that of the professoriat, into whose ranks I have made and unmade a number of forays.

There was a time, though, when at least in my guise as author (never mind its inseparability from that as hunter) I might expect toleration, if not support, from colleagues in the academy. It now seems as difficult to persuade trend-setting university critics, however, of literature's coherence or its claims on truth as to persuade them of such qualities in pursuing wild game. They speak no more of literature at all, only texts, a term not meant to be honorific; at the same time, of course, it is from texts alone that they have even their skimpy impressions of nature's business.

Life, though, is too short to preach to the literally ignorant, who cannot, *will* not be converted. So back to the real subject here. No matter how marginal any current writer's works may be, however, devalued or ingeniously misconstrued, I know this about my own: they depend on the austerity of autumn or winter. Quaint or not, I've said I'm stalking clarity, and the stalk demands a different ambience from stifling, crowded summer's.

Even mud season isn't bad. Sitting at my desk, I can at least look all the way to the bony ridge at the top of the mountain; and better mud, anyhow, than the veil of July leaf and vine and bush that, as I draft this, cuts off my view of that easterly ridge, and of so much else. Far better even the moribund snow and ice than, for instance, this seminar of wasps—a dozen strong and waxing— who bumble into one another on my windowsill. Better a slight shiver than the dozy fog I feel, behind that oven door of a window.

And yet.

And yet my testimony owes itself to old belief, as if a certain dream still actually lived: myself some unfettered Natty Bumpo, braving the chilly elements of upper New England in the days before the useless boutiques, before sushi was served up at parties in renovated farmhouses, before you saw some self-important jerk in a Volvo yammering into his cellular phone while waiting for the new traffic light to go green.

Truth is, once upon a time I did hate summer, and my imagination still clings to that hatred. But if a landscape can change, so can a truth. And it has. Or was it ever true? I try to answer and fail; but I no longer blame my uncertainty on summer vagueness, nor ask, contentiously: How can a person think when it's so damned hot?

In a poem I published some years back, I refer to myself as "the dull bourgeois I would have despised." That's what I am, for better or worse. I believe—shame!—it's for the better. So does the poem, which despite its melancholy goes on to applaud the friendliness of all the familial flesh around me, to celebrate the backyard barbecue (oh horror!) that I and an eight-year-old daughter ineptly wrought one summer, its mortar so sloppily mixed that after a single season the whole affair began to crumble.

My ghostly Natty still craves a spare and chilly surround in order to make him decisive, clear, and he still finds that craving countered by the soft-edged, billowy hazes of July and August; by everything that crumbles; by all that consigns itself to heap and sprawl. But my dull bourgeois suspects, however reluctantly, that summer—loose and silly though it be—may permit him to have it both ways. Provided he will let it.

Doubtless, the bourgeois rationalizes. And yet there *is*, finally, all that light! If Natty needs the cool breeze, he can go to the ridge and get it at 5:30 in the morning, the sun well up. Then he can tumble lazily downhill into all that clutter, and become someone else.

Just so, I daily descend to my grass-choked yard. To my one retired gun dog, all matt and drool and devotion, incapable of making the climb with the others anymore. To my wife, of whom I think with such pleasure and excitement that I'd feel mischievous to speak of her here in fuller detail. To my children, the younger ones sleeping as late as they like, the prospect of school remote enough for now to be unimaginable. From the smallest girl rushes a cascade of words and near-words, sounds she has no reason yet to force into meaning or pattern.

Those hay bales weren't so heavy, were they? That endless lull till the first autumn day, thrilling and anxious at once, in class-room and playground—there was a honey, after all, in such endlessness, wasn't there? And I must confess it's a miracle, the way these spiders stitch the woods, tree to tree to tree. Those are connections too. I can't know their relation to the more mystical ones I've always been after, but I know I needn't much strain to find them.

Unreasonable Bitch

M Y YOUNG DOG and I moved cross-lots through landscape she may well have seen that day; but I was
looking at much of it for the first time. Good country
too. The sun lay on the home side of the mountain by now, its
tawn faintly rimming the jackspruce uplands behind us. We struck
a year-round brook, whose waters showed nearly black at this
hour, though here and there a riffle blinked with the same tawny
luster. Even the fall-bleached ferns on the banks vaguely flickered.
I palmed a drink—wonderful, cool, sweet.

Strange territory, but I wasn't lost, not physically. I walked in
the opposite direction from my house only because I felt unequal
to climbing the mountain again. I'd skirt it instead, till I broke
onto the tote trail below Boulder City, then follow down to our
dirt road and cut back this way once more. Slow as the limp made
me, I'd still see my family before true dark.

Meanwhile, for all my tiredness and lameness, I felt easy in
our travel. A sort of order had been unskewed, even if to say so is
itself to skew matters somewhat, obscuring as I define. For the
God who made upper New England was no classicist, but found
charm in abrupt change: earlier October's glad rags, put on and
doffed almost at once, had become this week's somber oakleaf
and the comely pall of beech. First snow no doubt in the offing.
Warbler to junco to jay, legfur white on the hares, a flat-top
moon.

Wandering from a tall grove of evergreen through a clot of
bare alder, into a glade of withering Canada lily, across a hum-

mock quilled with hornbeam—stone and turf and swamp—I indistinctly imagined some great Protean beast, its sinews bunched for one moment, stretched in the next, looped or bowed or angled at whim. But drawn as much by the trivial as the mythic, I silently recited that old verse about how we should all be happy as kings, the world so full of a number of things.

"I've never owned a bad dog."

My words, aloud, spontaneous, had sounded small a quarter-hour ago in the unfamiliar woods where at last I found my new pointer Sue. Trees loomed high there by our boreal standards, blessed with south exposure and an atypical run of ledge-free soil.

I saw a vulture coast from its perch on a middle limb, then laze into flight. Loner.

Two barred owls, out of view among loftier boughs, responded to my phrase with apparent laughter. Never a bad dog? I hadn't felt that way for most of the afternoon, Sue absent without leave.

It's already clear this whole episode arrived at its happy ending. Still, truth lay with the owls, my emotions beforehand having approached the murderous. I'll admit as much not only for candor's sake but also lest I assign fault for her unruliness exclusively to the pointer. On the other hand, the fault wasn't mine alone either. Though I'm the one to claim it, and though my training habits strike many as haywire, I'm a more than fair handler of gun dogs—as I should be, if long experience is indeed a teacher.

Since I like hard-going, high-nosed, aggressive hunters, however, and am more apt to be urging them on than standing them on a table or constantly bleating *Whoa*, it's natural that a young prospect will get away from me now and then in early phases, mistaking my encouragement to boldness for absolute license. But better such a misjudgment than the opposite; I can't bear a timid worker.

Eventual success lies in combining a pointer's own confident instincts with my more pedestrian, human desire to be pleased. For verification of that pleasure, though, he or she needn't so much as break stride until coming on game. All I ask is that the dog check in every so often. Respectful friendship between us is the key, and such a relation requires plenty of time to establish.

But time was exactly what Sue and I didn't get.

I had another bitch just then, as fine a grouse dog as anyone will ever see. At five, right in her prime, Bessie did all I could ask. No sniffling. No self-doubt. No sheepish surrender, that is, to the gentleman birdshooter's lust for "hunting close." From the moment I uncrated her, she kept grouse on her mind far more than she did me; but we both benefitted hugely from that concentration. Bessie simply sailed through covers large and small, wasting no time with unfresh scent, keeping her pace till she struck something good and hot. And even then, she moved with assurance, till at last she locked on her bird.

That's the style for me, because although these many years should have made me an expert shot, the equivalent of a .330 batter in baseball, I'm afraid I'm that only in spurts: a streak hitter, you could say, who'll whiff on six consecutive pitches, then hammer a subsequent few. I need whatever advantages I can get. Over the years I've put a fat charge of grouse meat in the freezer, but only because I've had more than my share of those advantages. Some good dog has always coached me into position, has as it were stolen a bird's sign before the bird could deliver.

But here, confusing wild game with some human game, however noble, my analogies falter. Naked facts would serve more eloquently, if only I could find a logical way to present them. My lessons afield, however, persistently break my small logic down. In any case, no dog ever helped me better than Bess; or rather, I never offered my own petty help to a better dog than she. It's still a thrill to recall details: the upheld head, the fluent musculature, the tail on the vertical. "High at both ends," in the dog handler's phrase.

How beautiful, and how surprising in its way—for lounging in her run or sprawled on a cushion in my office, Bessie looked like no one's idea of a champion. My wife jokingly called her Yard Dog, after those hound-mix mongrels conspicuous in any impoverished province: one end of a chain is fixed to a gnawed stake in the hardpan, the other to the desolate beast, all rib and scale and whipworm.

And I smile to remember Bessie drinking from a stream on a certain warm October afternoon. The current is full of light and music, the encroaching knolls antic with color. The dog's tail has been thrashed hairless among the briar canes; she pokes it between her legs and along her belly, then lowers her somewhat snipey face to the water. How like a rat, I think. How very like a rat.

To repeat, though, Bessie at work was all the loveliness a dog could be. Her emphatically unratlike character somehow showed in her very design, conceived as I sometimes imagined by an intelligence too grand and original for my wit to comprehend. I'd often all but forget that a particular stance signified nearby prey: the point, so to speak, became the point, less a means than a glorious end in itself—like a revelation, an avatar. And although of course I always flushed and fired, that brilliant posture has lodged itself in mind more deeply than the deftest shot I ever made. If the same is true in some measure of each fine pointer I've trained, Bessie remains somehow quintessential. To see her disabled felt therefore like quintessential pain.

Late one summer, she developed what I believed an ordinary cough. Agreeing, my veterinarian—Walter Cottrell of Newbury, Vermont—put her on a course of antibiotics. Then another. Then others still. The hack, however, eventually punctuated by retching, persisted until Walt's diagnosis changed: kennel cough became chronic allergic bronchitis, which sounds specific enough but is in fact woefully blurry. Had Bessie inherited the disease or lately contracted it? What was the allergen, or was there more than one? Did it (or they) exist in her home environment?

Fearing this last possibility, I spent hours on hands and knees, dusting every book on my remotest office shelves, as if, to avenge my neglect of them, minor poets or no-longer-modish French essayists had released uncanny germs into our small domain. I scoured the concrete slab in Bessie's run, the plywood walls and floor in her house, every linoleum inch in the tiny bathroom where I kept her water dish. I hauled away the sorry couch on which she and other dogs had lain for decades.

But the trouble lingered toward the grouse season. I heard a cough in my dreams, rough and dry as stubblefields, and then a frothy, feckless vomiting.

Prognosis shifted with diagnosis: after consultation with a Cornell specialist, Dr. Cottrell warned me to hope for no more than

Bessie's partial return to capacity. Aided by steroids, perhaps she'd work a few hours at a time, provided I could rest her between hunting days, not to mention bird covers. And I mustn't raise pups by her.

I'd pondered breeding Bessie to my other pointer, Max, assuming he turned out as well as I hoped. A big male, but nearly a puppy himself at the time of all this, he'd had little more than yard training; yet I already liked how he moved, and even how conventionally handsome he was. I'd seen a host of pointers, including the beautiful Elhews from whose stock Max descends, but never a more striking specimen than he. In short, I had high expectations for the fellow. By the time they fulfilled themselves, however, I'd be finding him another wife.

Yet the more immediate worry still lay in those fast approaching grouse months. Walt urged me not to react dizzily. Perhaps Bessie's response to medication would be so positive that we could keep cutting the dosage even as her performance reverted as closely as possible to peak. Hold off, he counseled, before tracking down a new dog. He knew how my mind was turning.

Yet although he's a bird hunter too, my doctor friend likely didn't understand where my soul stood. Who on earth could, if I can't myself? I will later theorize—no more than that—on why a handful of days in the field will never do for me, or on why the older I get the harder it seems to imagine a fall of such casual hunting, let alone of none. Just now I'll recall only that these deprivations seemed alarmingly possible: for different reasons, neither Max nor Bessie stood ready for day after day of hard grousing.

I must shoot abundantly over my own dogs as some hard cases must smoke a lot of cigarettes. Moderation seems out of the question, and withdrawal so painful—the world without nicotine so oddly empty—that they persist in a habit that may well wreck their health. Of course, I hope this is only half accurate, since I've always considered my addiction life-enhancing rather than the opposite. At all events, emotionally as well as practically I needed a bird dog who could go full steam from opening morning, mere weeks away, till the last Friday before deer season, when afternoons would turn dark entirely.

Bessie had come to me as a puppy from a breeder in west Texas. Certain grouse hunters marvel that I favor pointers at all, the American strain having been developed primarily for quail in the flatlands, where humans follow in Jeeps or on horseback. That I should choose from a *Texan* line—its grande dame moreover one Rebel Hawk, a renowned galloper—strikes them as original insanity emphasized.

Their assumption is that in pursuit of birds so jumpy as New England grouse you must sneak along behind more deliberate continentals—Brittany spaniels, German shorthairs, Griffons, and so on—or, if you have a taste for mild adventure, regionally bred English setters. My view is simply this: the American pointer is the best gun breed in history. For me, that alone should close the case. Since it's folly to imagine sneaking up on a grouse anyhow, one is better off with a dog who charges right at the bird, thereby, as my experience suggests, pinning him into a fastness he rarely shows to potterers. And of course it makes greater sense to run a dog who will now and then bump a grouse (as which one of which breed won't?) in the course of *finding* so many more than a sniffer will ever do. If your pointing animal stays close enough that he or she needn't even be called now and then, why not buy a flush dog and forget the whole controversy?

None of this touches, of course, on the undeniable superiority of a pointer's style.

Yet I'm not out to convert anybody. I know that one creature's wisdom is another's madness, and that it's for reasons other than reason itself that I cling to my opinions and superstitions. They seem blessedly justified by the likes of Bessie, yes. But more importantly, they help sustain a personal narrative that I've been composing all my life.

Having arrived at an unexpected interruption of that narrative, I called the same Texan breeder. I wanted a bitch, I explained. And I wanted one old enough to keep an arduous regimen but not "finished" by another handler, not set in her ways. To begin with, conditions are utterly different in upper New England from those in the breeder's territory: a sidehill grouse tangle is no more the vast, open land of the southwest than a grouse itself is a quail. My new dog had to be birdy, as they say, had to possess a keen pointing instinct together with plenty of drive; but her harder training must still lie ahead of her. If in my wretched circumstance I was looking for a pointer who'd been introduced to wild fowl, I also sought one on whom I could still have influence, and on whom my region and game could make larger impressions, as they do, covers and quarry marvelously insinuating themselves into a good dog's sense of the world.

We settled on such a "started" animal, and I soon drove up to the Burlington airport to meet her.

With her full chest and the perpendicular meeting of her brow and muzzle, Sue represented her breed more classically than poor Bessie, though she had her distinctions too, chiefly the band of solid liver extending almost the length of her tail, a marking I'd never seen in another pointer. For all her vigorous appearance, however, she was skittish as a mink when I picked her up, and for a good while after. Had she come from somewhere else, I might in fact have imagined an abusive prior owner.

On the trip back, as so often, I blessed the presence of the good animal doctor, Walt Cottrell, who'd ridden with me despite the wee-hour landing of the plane from Austin and the long road trek. Walt's knack for soothing his patients ranks high among his many enviable clinician's tricks, though these are probably both less clinical and tricky than I make them sound. He kept a gentle hand on the trembling youngster all the way home, and I dropped him off with some trepidation. Happily, Sue seemed reassured by the proximity of my other dogs in their runs. She settled immediately, and so did I, into a dreamful sleep: puckerbrush; birds; yellow maples; puddle ice; pommacey air.

Never before had such dreams come too rapidly true for my liking. But now I actually ached to defer the white-grass mornings of grouse season, so laden with uncertainty this year. Of course they dawned on me anyhow, all in a rush. To my delight, however, Bessie's medication (or perhaps something more uncanny) took sudden hold. She put on flesh. Her cough went into remission. Surely the time had passed when I could run her and her only, say, for seven straight and demanding days, but I now hoped that by middle autumn I'd be trading some of her covers—and if necessary some of her full hunts—to her lately arrived kennelmate.

This might prove a more than satisfactory arrangement: my veteran for pure skill and results, my newcomer for the challenge presented by any young prospect.

That challenge proved more than I'd bargained for. I've said that conditions deprived Sue and me of leisurely, proper acquaintance. She showed up, she skated around my office for a while, and then we headed outdoors; but we both soon got bored (Sue more than I) with our few dull drills within the chainlink of the village ballfield.

A more rational man would perhaps have progressed from there to a wider field, without such unnatural bordering. But I make no claims to rationality here. Or anywhere. Just the contrary.

I quickly learned that within a fence my new dog was biddable as a blind person's guide, but that one knoll or thicket between us made her into a whippet on stimulants. Pawn to my own philosophy, however, I put on a show, if only to myself, of affirming her very explosiveness. She'd learn to govern all that fire—the woods and the birds would teach her—but she'd never be, in my friend Landy Bartlett's phrase, a vacuum cleaner, more likely to trip me up than to find much game. True enough, I was meanwhile doing a lot of *dog* hunting, even as I hunted birds almost as little as I'd earlier feared.

Compensation lay in what few hours I could devote to grouse in my older pointer's company, worth seasons in any other's. I've watched all my gun dogs turn red hot for stretches, when they seemed not only capable of finding each bird in each of the three states I roam but also of holding each till I or a partner had every chance a grouse hunter could plausibly (or implausibly) ask; but that fall my poor ill Bessie simply stuck at that level, never a middling day.

Struggle with Sue seemed a modest enough price for such luxury; indeed, it sounded wrong to call it a price at all. This was scarcely the first year I'd run a mere tyro even while I had an able, mature alternative on hand—Bessie herself, for instance, back when Annie showed her best. I've implied that much of autumn's savor for a real hunter comes of its challenge; as the autumns accumulate, the better and better part of challenge lies for me in handling dogs.

And Sue and I, having already killed a few birds together in the proper fashion, were making undeniable progress . . . despite her yen, more sporadic with the passing days but still not totally quenched, to leave me, my teeth in my mouth.

"There is gone," my pal Joey Olsen once suggested, "and there is *gone*." Sue knew about both modes of disappearance, the second perhaps better than the first.

❦

I must now turn to a dreadful development, which I'll do as curtly as I can, so as not to lapse—with a hindsight that according to the old lie is 20-20—into mourning, remorse, and self-rebuke. On a certain cold noon, after she'd rested for nearly a week, I took Bessie out for a ramble in my best cover. Or *her* best cover, I should say, since for many years I'd been ignorant of its birdiest sectors; Bessie led me to them, ranging one day to a may-apple orchard on the far side of some tall timber. For all I can testify, she'd known about that sprawling stand for a long time; but I hope not, because if so I'd deprived her of using her knowledge for several seasons by whistling her back, routinely, from the unpromising bigwoods this side of it.

One ought never to settle for routine, not when hunting quick-witted game with a quick-witted dog.

I ought right along to have let Bessie go—as I did on this later day, when she appeared fitter than she had all fall, when there seemed as many grouse as haws among the feed bushes, when against the still-white understorey the world was everywhere scarlet fruit and glittering leafless branch and mottled wing. And among and above all, a pointer streaking and halting, genius of the place.

Unless I dream now, the birds were coveyed like southland bobwhite. They exploded in unthinkable numbers at a time; but Bessie went on unrattled. At one stage, a dead grouse already in her mouth, she locked on a second, which had crouched in brush behind a mouldering old woodpile, the air all asquiggle above it, like air you might see in slumber or fever. My dog watched as I shot that second grouse, brought the first back to me, then proceeded to retrieve the other.

I claim no similar poise in myself: aside from my small contribution to the achievement just mentioned, I put in a mediocre afternoon, to say it kindly. I'd have cursed my bad aim over Sue, who still needed the feel in her jaws of a grouse she'd found and held. Indeed, it may have been fear of my own poor gunning that kept me from going home for the younger pointer, from bringing her back to this plenty. Bessie was too much the professional to be corrupted or distracted by my bungling, but with an inexperienced dog it's important to make shots count.

There was, however, a truer motive for staying on. Not to shoot a limit, as I finally, falteringly did. No. Piling up a kill seemed less than inconsequential compared to my older bitch's glorious work. Simple greed to watch that work held me in our thorn orchard. And though I would later lament having done so for too long, I try now to believe that greed—if the word must stand—can show a noble form, one creature taking vast personal pleasure in his witness of another's.

I try moreover to believe that my dog and I both knew this hunt might be among our *last* splendors together. I no more voiced a word than she did; but we spoke of final things. Truth was in the air—along with the thunder of grouse, the tang of frost and fretted apple.

❦

When I came out of the house to see her next morning, Bessie looked terrible, tremulous, lethargic. Hearing the nightmare cough for the first time in more than a month, I immediately phoned the vet, who came and gave her a steroid injection, together with an antibiotic, just to be safe. The steroids, without which she could scarcely breathe, also suppressed her immune systems, and Walt didn't want to risk opportunist bacterial invasion.

A week or two later, once our nerves had settled some, I would say, "I think I imagined this, way back in summer."

"I bet you did," Walt replied, "And that kind of imagination is *always* right."

For in spite of us all it had come, the bacterial invasion, leaving behind it a weight I still feel . . . and an unreliable character named Sue—to whom for all sorts of reasons I'll return here till I'm done.

It's time in fact for a return to the particular afternoon when this story began, or seemed to begin. Bessie was still alive then, which is partly why I often wondered at my own behavior. For despite my suggestions till now to the contrary, Sue frequently made it hard to sort challenge from impossibility, a yen for refreshment from perversity. And never more so than on that day: hour upon hour, as I futilely listened for her, I asked myself stiff questions. Who is his right mind would spend so much time during the very bird season working such a prospect? Who would thereby sacrifice other time, however limited, with a gun dog no less than ideal? Who but a madman?

Some sources of the madness were doubtless inscrutable, but I'm certain of one. Since the only thing I ever regret about the bird season is the October ending of another season, I happened to be reading a baseball book just then. Somehow, perhaps a bit like grouse hunting—and unlike, for example, football, a game that bores me stupid—baseball attracts me by interfusing action and meditation. In Donal Honig's *Baseball When The Grass Was Green*, I came on some comments by the old Dodger outfielder Peter Reiser, one of whose famous collisions with the Ebbetts Field wall occurred in a 1942 contest with the Cardinals. Asked why he did not go easier on himself, given his team's thirteen-and-a-half-game lead, Reiser replied: "You can't. You slow up half a step and it's the beginning of your last ball game. You can't turn it on and off any time you want to."

The player's words had an authoritative ring. Deny it as I might, my hours of chasing grouse would soon enough be limited by something besides ageing pointers. There was no call to help the process along. My almost fifty autumns had not greatly sapped my energy, but that very fact ratified a Reiserian belief—the best way to keep doing what you love to do is exactly to keep doing it, hard. To settle for less in this season will be to settle for less in the next and next. Thus for all the apparent craziness and the genuine pain involved, I regarded my recent attempts to run down a fast pointer in steep country as proof that time hadn't touched my old pig-headed self.

Of course I couldn't, then or ever, truly run a quick dog down. Strategy and lucky guesswork came into play. At one point that afternoon, I managed to position myself behind a boulder as Sue charged my way down a dry brookbed. I meant to cut her off, to show her who was boss out here. But her reactions proved the livelier by far: startled by my leap, she stomped her throttle and flashed past.

Having nothing to show beyond a rock-bunged knee and a rope burn from the check cord I couldn't quite seize, I lay there in the evergreen straw for what is aptly called a spell. The racket of a woodpecker far down in bottomland sounded gradual, dreamy. I followed the languid progress of a cloud, eastward toward next day. The Indian summer breeze softly jostled a hemlock, in whose top I could just discern the tatters of a raven's nest.

As my sweat cooled, I made a vow to hold this mood, in which everything seemed at once brand new and familiar. I'd never been in these woods, and had. That pileated woodpecker, somewhere pouring down his square-wrought chips of gold: I was listening to him for the first time; yet he was also every woodpecker of every species I'd heard from childhood. The slim cloud overhead, although so random and ephemeral, was still an emblem of the many times in a fortunate life I'd lolled and beheld a country sky—as I could go on doing for as long as ambition lasted. That ragged nest overhead recalled a morning when I climbed a pine on my uncle's farm to steal a hatchling crow for a pet. As I ducked the plunges of the screaming hen, the treetop swung back and forth with my weight. That sway terrified a ten-year-old, but lying by the brook I could almost feel it again, and it seemed cradlelike.

Surely the greatest virtue in doing what one has long done is that these instants do transpire, past, present, and future becoming somehow seamless. Experience, momentarily purged of unease, looks impervious to change, no matter the countervailing evidence. Deaths of heart's companions, human and otherwise. Ruin of cherished places. Tenacity of human stupidity, which of all things truly endures—my own was recouping even then.

I'm not sure what snapped me out of reverie and back to a world exactly of wholesale alterations, to the recognition for example that as a younger fellow I'd likely have walked it off in a few strides, my minor limp from the vain dive at Sue's check cord. Picking grit from my palms, I also realized that there wouldn't have *been* a check cord back then. The imagination operates by virtue of such ordinary detail, memories coalescing in unexpected ways.

Whether imagination soothes or troubles, however, whether it entrances or sobers—that is a different issue.

I recalled that I'd had my battles even with the noble Bessie, a less headstrong runner than Sue but still a runner. Till now, however, I'd never resorted to a check cord. No more than the overlong leash that many a trainer uses to steady his dogs on released birds, the cord had always smacked too much of the "hunt close" obsession, had flown in the face of my opinionation.

"I don't plan to go gunning for pen birds," I'd sneer.

The idea, I argued, was to put a dog on the quarry you expected to find in the wild: if he or she bumped that quarry or broke point on it, you chased the dog down, dragged it back, stood it on the spot where the error had taken place. Success with such an approach, needless to say, demanded that I know plenty of country in which to work native game; but I've always been good for that, however much off-season exploration or in-season travel the knowledge requires, and—since I will not shoot a bird unless a dog has been the one to find it—however much restraint.

Still, on the afternoon I speak of, driven by Sue's hard-headedness and by the exigencies of time, I'd already departed from a number of my former convictions. I'd begun taking her into territory where I *doubted* there'd be game, not only because such a condition can sometimes present itself in the most productive cover, but also because more than any other it frequently caused Sue's unruliness. Frustrated, she'd depart for some faraway place where she could hope to find birds on her own. If the game were thick enough, she posed no problem; if it were scarce,

I sometimes had a long wait till I saw her again. My object now was to break such a formula, enforcing self-control under all circumstances. To do so I needed now and then to intercept her, and for all of me, a check cord seemed a necessary tool.

By that afternoon, having proved effective enough in recent weeks, the method seemed one I might soon quit. I hoped so, right to my bones, for the cord shamed me, suggesting how much of my prior opinion had been mere bumptiousness. I winced to recall my radical advice in an old magazine article: "If you have a check cord, burn it." So long as I regarded my current behavior as exceptional, I could see temporary compromise in it rather than diminishment or hypocrisy.

But I was diminished and hypocritical in any case. For I'd also, Lord save me, put an electronic beeper collar on Sue, so that I could know her whereabouts or, if she stayed too long out of earshot, I could find the place where her rope had caught on brush.

How tarnished, the whole business! My loathing for a check cord may have been equivocal enough, but there were solid reasons to wince at using a beeper to keep track of a dog among heavy brush, rather than the traditional brass bell. In the sound from such a simple bell, perhaps precisely because it does represent tradition, I hear a congruity with the sacred woods of autumn; but the opposite is true of anything electronic. I disappear into those woods in part to *abandon* the electrified, gadgety world and all its inorganic noise—which means that a beeper belongs in the same category as the fishfinder, the battery-driven trolling motor, the radio transmitter borne by modern-day bear hounds.

Let creeping Nintendoism not creep into certain quarters, I say; let a little space remain essential.

There were moments when I swore I actually saw the collar's electric waves, writhing like weird mechanical serpents, loathsome less for their odd venom—which had, so to say, its medicinal properties—than for their being so damned out of place in our snakeless, unmachined fall covers. Yet I had to live with such dismaying fancies, given an insuperable defect in a mere bell;

namely, that once Sue stopped going, so would its clapper. In-deed, just as a virtue of brass is that its tune indicates a moving dog, another is that the tune's absence indicates an unmoving one. I'm excited even to write of such silence, toward which I have so often hastened in heart-stirring expectation of a point, and of racketing wings that would break the quiet.

But to teach Sue that, bolt as she might, or even hide, I would always at length discover her; that punishment was therefore inevitable; that the wisest course was simply not to take off in the first place—to do all that, I needed a locator that would go on operating whether the dog was running or tied against her will to root or sapling or stone. Otherwise, unless she barked, I'd have no way on earth or tracking her down.

There were therefore risks to more than self-esteem in my new approach. Although the beeper's wretched signal carried well, it could not penetrate miles of hardscrabble woods or granite-capped knolls. Once Sue truly got away on me, it could take a hell of a lot of tramping in every direction till I came on her. Often enough I imagined a garrotting, or, since the collar operated on batteries, a lingering death by starvation, the beeps gone mute.

I must confess that despite my calm interval by the brook, I half-wished the damn bitch *would* go hang herself that afternoon. For a time I entered a mood that, if unchecked, poses dangers almost as severe to the handler-and-dog relationship as death itself; I'd begun to resent Sue for not being . . . reasonable. I think back and shudder, thankful for the many hours that allowed me to get over such silliness, for the moderate but deafening wind that for all I can say allowed me to charge past the pointer several times before finding her at last—on the far, the unfamiliar side of our mountain.

To have come on Sue sooner, in near and well-known country, might have been a catastrophe. For half the afternoon I stormed the woods like a bad wind myself. What in hell was wrong with this goddamned animal? Didn't she know how fortunately she'd landed, treated with a personal attention that no large-scale train-er could spare time for, yet exposed to more hunting than she could dream of with some weekender? Rather than being cooped up in a run when she was *not* hunting, she could lie by the woodstove in my office, or else join in my long daily rambles through landscape devoid of any traffic but our own.

And hadn't she felt the goodness of those times when she'd done everything right, when we were teammates instead of adversaries, when she held her point, heard my Winchester's blast, tasted the mouthful of warm feathers? Wasn't it obvious how slightly she needed to adjust her impulses in order to have all that, again and again?

§

This essay does not aim for suspense, so I'll say that in time— indeed, by the tail end of that very season—Sue would prove every bit the prospect I'd craved. Come winter I would look back with satisfaction even on that afternoon's ordeal, claiming as ever that it's better to have a volatile dog than one you must labor to ignite. Sue would maintain the drive she'd always shown, but it would at last come under appropriate control. More hers, happily, than mine—she would not, in short, accept my notions of reason, but discover her own, with however much or little of my help.

Yet now, looking back again, I doubt that the very concept of rationality has any place among these musings. In so saying, I don't mean to raise the endless issue of whether a so-called lower animal possesses such a faculty. Whatever it is that accounts for a good bird dog's intelligence, it cannot be named in human terms, and if it could, the semantics wouldn't get us far in any case. I know only what I've said—that it would have been ruinous that day for my perfectly reasonable irritation to prevail; and I know that a good share of my retrospective gratitude is due in the end to an unreasonable bitch, who would not let it do so.

No, nothing rational led me through and *out of* my many anthropomorphizing prejudices, all too damnably familiar. Perhaps like any modern I need those prejudices, but in the calm of reflection I consider myself the better for doing without them now and then, for moving into unfamiliar ground, as by the close of that galling day I'd done. Literally and otherwise. That stretch of big forest where I finally came on Sue, her cord wrapped on an upthrust hemlock root, was not so distant from my house; yet I'd never seen its insides. I knew where it lay on the map, but I hadn't *been* there. Anything could happen.

As if to prove as much, after unknotting the pointer, by some instinct or intuition, I turned my eyes upward. That vulture perched just above, as in some banal wild west film. "Not today," I muttered, accepting the banality, despising the ugly creature. But suddenly I smiled, less in amusement than approval: the vulture was all a vulture should be: ardent, patient, incredibly keen-sighted, and graceful beyond words as it swooped from its bough, then made for the far ridge's dying shimmer. Beautiful.

Oh, I'd worked hard enough today, but what interesting work. And somewhere it all made the same sort of beautiful sense as that great bird. I was no madman. I neither squandered nor hoarded time. I didn't know my Bessie was dying, and yet I must have. There were forces involved that couldn't be defined by me, any more than by Bessie herself—Bessie, who had taken me farther into wondrous places than the majority of contemporary human-kind is blessed to go, farther than my own self-generated explorations would ever have led me, places where reason's unreasonableness seems manifest.

And now another dog would do the same, already had.

On the Bubble

EARLY JUNE OF 1992, below Stonehouse Mountain, Grafton County, New Hampshire—a place and time in which snowsqualls, routine enough just weeks ago, will at last deserve the name freakish. In freshet beds where waters flared and vanished, frail shoots of jewelweed declare themselves; grass bursts the voles' winter tunnels; geese trail the Connecticut northward; the buck deer's antlers are in velvet; the woodchuck's busy to double in weight; trout sip the ponds' ephemerids; everywhere, the lovesick insistence of birds.

Our family has lived ten years on this foothill's flank, but soon after dawn this morning—beckoned by the full day ahead—I hiked down from its mild summit for perhaps the last time. The ramble, especially under such circumstances, brought back the many I'd made there, in company or alone, one recollection summoning another, and that one still another, till outward prospects opened onto vaster, more labyrinthine inward views.

I suddenly found myself at the June of 1989, three years gone. Unseasonable as any late spring's for a hunt, that forenoon had still invited my scout's eye; for companions therefore I had my gun dogs, two of them dead since. And because I'm also forever scouting more than game—no easy name for it—I'd also brought along my third-born, Jordan. He'd turned five less than a month before; I would manage to haul him in his riding pack through one more year.

As soon as we struck height-of-land, my boy reached into his jacket and fetched out paraphernalia for blowing bubbles. What few he managed were pea-sized and, hustled by a hard wind, quickly burst against the granite moraine where we stood. Jordan, however, is more stubborn a soul than I will ever quite understand, no matter that, despite its costs, I share the quality myself, in spades. For all my untypically rationalistic discouragement, he persisted until in a momentary lull he somehow produced one outsized sphere. Perhaps six inches around, it lifted off his dipper, fighting like a hot-air balloon for altitude—which it couldn't sustain. As my son watched in an agony between rage and sorrow, the great thing sank slowly toward stone. On lighting, though, it remained miraculously intact—tenuous, quivering. I could actually hear the catch in Jordan's breath as he beheld in its film the reflections of a whole domain: high blue crossed by thunderheads, skinny black upland spruces, weathered crags and windfalls, glyphs of animal trails.

He and I would miss all this directly.

Then the bubble vanished. No obvious pop, only evanescence. And in the after-moment, by quenchless habit I began to conjure metaphors. The perdurability of the mountain, the transience of human constructs, the rest. But all sorts of things—inner and outer, gross and subtle—blocked my scheme, and I gave it up. If I've discovered nothing else, I know that one can't simply will his figures.

Besides, there seemed enough in the plain spectacle of the child, dazed by these quicksilver splendors and their disappearance, to cause a familiar commotion. I was moved by more than his mere smallness, the puff of his bewildered lips, the way his pale, forgotten hand spilled the bubble-jar's contents. I felt, almost physically, the curse fallen on his parents' wish for him and his sisters and brothers: that we might leave these young spirits among the apparent unchangeables that had nourished our own—this wish in fact had moved us all to Stonehouse Mountain, whose very name seemed auspicious. Between eternities of stone and mountain, a house might nestle for good.

Not that I'd left my former town, some miles to the south, altogether cheerfully, having cherished it so for the preceding decade and a half. Yet after that time, I watched the village and its surroundings transform themselves, overnight it seemed, into a sprawl of bedrooms for the burgeoning college-and-commercial cluster downriver. The jobs—far scarcer in actuality than in developers' fabulations—had arrived and departed so quickly that, on looking one day, I found native families gone, their farms become "grounds."

Eighty-year-old Harry Franklin, among the few who stayed, put matters succinctly: "We're just like anyplace else now."

☙

This morning's reverie on my son's bright bubble must have established a motif of fragile glories, that motif in turn leading to further recollections, which otherwise seem willy-nilly, or at least nonchronological. I shortly found myself leaping to the autumn of 1991. That was a fall like many another in obvious respects: fragile, yes—flares of maple racing into the umbers and beiges of oak or beech; short summer shadows stretched suddenly long after noontime; big-fingered ferns gone arthritic as the swamps showed the first pale ice at their margins. But even more than usual, I'd been out and busy. From the final weekend of September till the middle one in November, I chased birds pretty much every day. Nasty work, of course, but necessary: my two youngest pointers were just at field training age. If, as usual, I lamented the headlong rush of those weeks, it was as much because the pups deserved more exposure than I could cram into a season as because of my ineradicable elegiac streak.

Therefore, when it came to deer season (which, precisely for being dogless, shakes less passion from me anyhow than the grouse months), I hunted too rarely and casually. But this was of necessity, too. A part of me would choose to spend as much time year-round in the wild as it had done all fall with the pointers, yet I must now and then come indoors, there to ponder other things: my children growing up; my wife ageing into a greater and greater handsomeness, in every sense of that word; reflections like these passing—so far as possible—into articulation.

In short, as the eleventh month of '91 advanced on the twelfth, I spared only an hour here and another there to follow the whitetail, preoccupied as I was with separate pursuits. Such an approach may reap results in places like Pennsylvania or Texas, but in my edge of New England—herd thinner, woods thicker— it's apt, barring dumb luck, to end in failure.

It did. It didn't.

𝕏

My first morning out was all Indian summer crackle underfoot, but by the second, several days later, conditions had turned ideal: a light snow fallen on unfrozen ground, sign would be clear, the going quiet. Moreover, though as always I'd cherished October's game more than the bigger game of the moment, there was and is something about November that exerts a stronger *aesthetic* appeal. I know that to say so puts me in a distinct minority, but the austerity of that period just before real snow—of sharply contoured branch and trunk, granite and cloud—oddly braces my soul.

I recall setting off in that second dawn at a brisk clip, which I meant to keep till I came on something interesting. This didn't take long: less than a mile from home, on a brushed-over twitch road at the north end of Stonehouse, I fairly struck a turnpike, deer tracks everywhere. Mostly skippers and does, of course, but one heel-heavy trail, too, fresh as paint, every third print ruddy with rut. I wondered for the hundredth time how a buck can manage to produce so much of that dribble—as if this were the chief internal mystery in such a creature.

There's a certain special outcropping on Stonehouse Mountain that, though short of the summit, provides as bold a view: the loftier Whites to northeastward in the distance, and—closer below—that bijou, Mason Pond. Flush with first settlement here, my wife and I happened onto this ledge in one of our early, desultory explorations. No sign of human presence around us or in the vista, we found it hard to suppose that a lone soul knew or remembered this corner of forest, which then belonged, technically, to an unknown out-of-stater. We spoke of rigging a sledge some winter, dragging materials to the site for a shack, even

installing our extra woodstove. Then we'd make occasional geta-
ways. If our cabin were found and dismantled, what harm? We'd
have had it for a spell anyway.

These musings preceded our small children. And someone else
soon bought that flank of mountain anyhow, for which he now
plans fifteen "luxury estates." Thus our musings turned to idle
dreams before we owned a prayer of making them otherwise, but
neither dream nor prayer will utterly die; we still name that spot
"The Shack." It stays on, somehow, as a place in mind. Yet how
can we pass such inner property down to those same children?

I'd been saying something else, however, before sorrow and
anger broke in. Taking the buck's track last fall, I shortly found
myself exactly at The Shack. Perhaps that very sorrow and anger
distracted me; in any case, I relaxed concentration as one so easily
does, and I missed my deer until too late. A good buck, right
enough. Although I couldn't count horns, of course, there looked
like a thicket of them as he bolted into softwood cover: I could see
that much, and the bulk of him, and the almost black color which
typifies our trophy ridge-runners. I could have shot—and would
have, in my youth—yet I knew that it would be no more than
luck if my slug hit, that it would go in from behind. It would ruin
a share of venison, and might do far worse: I'll haltingly acknowledge some atavistic excitement in following a blood trail—but
not a long one.

I performed an old charade of rage, complete with misdirected
oaths at the vanished prey: "Why, you son of a *bitch!* I'll fix *you!*"
But in truth I remained happy at my own calm and resignation;
I'd rest the fellow a spell and then pick him up again. Brushing
the scarf of snow from a blowdown, I sat and lit a pipe. When I
checked my watch, though, it astonished me as ever: two full
hours gone, all I'd allotted for this morning's chase. No, I
wouldn't fix that buck, not today. Instead I'd follow an arc down
to our house, semi-alert, just in case I jumped something else on
the way. But that would be accident, too, and in any case my
thoughts had already gone elsewhere.

The younger children must be getting up about now; it pleased
me to imagine them at a front window, frowzy, curious, and then
the sleep on their necks a warmth against my cold face. They'd

grow up so soon. The thought of my firstborn Creston, off at college just now, was bittersweet; how thoughtful and decent and *interesting* a man he'd become; yet how wouldn't I miss the vanished little boy in him? And the next child, Erika, was already fourteen, bright and beautiful.

I'd have stopped the whole lot in their tracks if I could, or maybe even moved them backwards in time—back to Jordan's age, or three-year-old Catherine's, or even to the age of the next tiny mystery, who'd arrive in his or her splendor a month from that deer-hunting day. I'd load each one by turns in the battered old pack, heft them, march them with me into the wonderful highlands. We'd see things together again.

❧

By a cellar hole in a certain burntland, an abandoned Model A lay for decades: we named the place Henry's Clearing, after the car's inventor. I have a picture of my oldest son astride the wreck's springless seat. He's ten. Beside him, a popple sapling has grown through the floorboards; it rests a feathery branch on the rust-orange dashboard, as a slim, slightly apprehensive adolescent girl might rest her fingertips. The skins of child and tree seemed translucent that morning and—far more than in the photograph —they remain that way to my interior eye.

Six months ago my big boy turned twenty. His companion popple is dead, scalped by the local developer when his crew removed the jalopy as an eyesore. One of his intended access roads will pass through the old burn. As I approached Henry's Clearing, I imagined gleaming foreign sedans, run hub-deep into March goo and left to replace the Model A. Such a fantasy made me grin—but only momentarily. Pavement would follow, sure as death.

Just east of Henry's, I froze—my impulse strange but familiar to anyone who's hunted long enough. I felt sure a deer stood somewhere near. Don't ask how. It couldn't have been my hearing, which is not worth much (and which forty years of shooting haven't improved). In my time, if children contracted ear infections, they went to a doctor and got them lanced. That fact is

worth remembering, perhaps, while I rhapsodize on bygone days:
I seem to have had those infections every other week, so my aural
channels are a maze of scar tissue. Even though my sons and
daughters appear equally susceptible to their father's old malady,
they will never, like him, confuse some inward clatter of the
eardrum with duck flight, some high whine through it with a
building wind, some uncertainly located pop with the far report
of a firearm. None will wonder, as I soon did near that burn,
whether an actual or illusory squelch sounded in dampening
snow.

I chose, at least for the moment, to believe in the sound's
reality, and I felt gratified once again that a belief could still make
my heart rap. I smelled an odor like the ozone warning of
electrical storm. My mouth went cotton. Slowly I settled my
backside onto a boulder, watching until my eyes teared and I had
no choice but to blink. Then I watched some more, shivering,
willing the deer of my intuitions around the shoulder of the knoll
and into Henry's Clearing—broadside, big. My younger son,
seven by now, could eat four chops at a go.

A different man would have waited even longer. I, however,
began in due course to doubt my own instincts, even if I'd had
reason to curse such reckless doubt in the past. But as I say, I had
home on the brain by now, and was unsure anyhow that I wanted
a buck I'd done so little to deserve, supposing he *were* on hand. As
the game thins out, its supporting habitat savaged by conspirators
in greed, a hunter should place demands on himself; he should do
things right or not at all.

In 1991, that ravenous seven-year-old fairly wriggled with enthusiasm for the woods and the quarry. Stuck unmoving to my
perch, I remembered the same fever from my childhood. With
him, flesh of my flesh, I could somehow chafe again for a first
armed trip to the field. I too could hang on a porch door, awaiting
a parent's return from his hunt. Then I could smell the cold dirt
on his dogs, the humid stench of birdfeathers in the gamebag. My
father would suffer my slow services: I could kneel and undo his
bootlaces, the aroma of man falling all over me.

It had only been four short decades before, after all, that I'd
done and felt these things. But when four more had passed, when

the boy had reached my age, when it was 2031, what of this sort would thrill him, in fact or imagination or memory? What would keep him watching as I watched, even as a chilly dampness climbed through pantswool into my bones? *Where* would he sit, and what would he pass on to his own children? What could I myself pass on—from here, from there?

I needed to disrupt my own mood, and so—the wind northwest, straight in my face—I decided to sneak over for a look through the burn, a mere twenty yards from my stand. I took most of that distance easy, a little at a time, eyeing the spot where I'd have to scooch to keep my profile under the slope's, injuries to each knee speaking more sternly now than in the sports-crazy boyhood that produced them.

Step, stop, wait. Step, stop, wait.

I flinched as a raven *whoof-whoof-whoofed* low overhead, across the fire-cleared ground and gone. The bird left a deeper quiet than the one it had broken, and I lingered within it till by God I did hear something! A small racket in brush around the corner. I sucked my teeth, trying to swallow but trying also to reason: if I'd heard a deer at all, odds favored a doe; or it might as easily turn out to be a plain old red squirrel, famous for disproportionate ruckus in a calm woods.

Five squatting steps further on, inch by inch I straightened. Over the knoll's rim, some forty yards down the former tote road, sure enough I detected fur and motion. A flag? No. Though I couldn't yet tell to what else, it belonged to no deer. Wrong color for a start: chocolate brown, highlit by cinnamon.

At length the animal slipped from brush and showed its shape entire. Still unable to identify it, I could see it was large. I stood fixed as a pillar while it made its unmistakable way toward me. The wind had picked up some, but kept moving toward me too. Better and better.

Then, something familiar but inexplicable: rather than growing bigger, my creature began to shrink as it came on. Noting the fussy lope of the weasel family, I thought: Well, I'll be damned, an otter! I'd happened on such apparent strays before, especially in the cold months, far from any watershed worth the name. Better and better.

Then I noticed the too-prominent ears, and I briefly imagined: *marten!* But this fellow, even as he got smaller, looked heavier than martens, which in any case, alas, had vanished from virtually all of New Hampshire some time ago. And yet since he is to the more common black as one to five, the pure-brown fisher—as he eventually became—proved no disappointment . . . especially as he kept up his nosey progress. The wind from behind him blew more insistently now: I could see backhairs ruffle like a field of late hay, and vague cloud-shadows skidding past on the coarse wet turf.

A good hound couldn't have smelled me from that animal's quarter; but just as the human, without any sensory clue, may occasionally surmise the nearness of the nonhuman, so now my fisher *felt* something out of the ordinary, stopped in his tracks, raised his head, sniffed the useless air.

We were in full sight of each other, but my eyes were the better. How many minutes, then, did we stand like that? One? Four? Ten? We stayed equally motionless, but my mind continued to run anyhow. And the fisher's? Were there images in his brain too, and if so, how did they look? How had it happened that a man could see his boy blow soap bubbles in another season and another niche of this very mountain, and still somehow be here this morning? Was my wife happy enough with our life together? Did the fisher believe he'd find hare in Henry's Clearing? Had he found them before? Did he store that experience? How? Was he in fact a she? Who had owned the Model A? Would anyone store memories of me? Did God really count each bird that fell and, having counted, what did He conclude? Why does blue show up under scarred paper birchbark like that tree's five yards to the animal's right? What made this particular scar? Did you feel the cold in Idaho, say, as you did in New England? Could a person go on fathering children and still complain about his world's crowding?

Perhaps I didn't think these exact thoughts just then. I mean to present less my mind's *content* than the way it kept filling with things apparently random and unaccountable. What had any to do with an outsized weasel, to whom I was about to wave or speak, excited as always to witness a wild thing's most frantic flight? No time to say. Suddenly, the big wind blew a gap in the overcast, and a filament of sun struck the fisher. The guard hairs of his coat became a numinous, gilded aura, I gasped, the cloud cover sealed itself again, the creature bounded into near woods, took to the treetops, leaping from one to another out of sight.

I stayed on for a spell, some bloodheat distracting me from weather's authority. But the wind soon gathered a few horizontal rainsplots, and I came to: my knuckles ached on the rifle, my wet bottom burned with the cold, and a gloom descended, which was instantaneous as the clouds' return and sadly common in my middle life. In what direction would my fisher's children fly, and my own, once the 'dozers had coughed and quit, the backhoes dug and gone?

Oh, I'd seen something that morning. I'd see it till my own dark hole got dug.

And after that?

꙾

The adored father who was my first guide died in the February of my twenty-third year. I married the following June, though my better soul found something wrong in taking such an important step while still gripped by a mourning so heavy and confusing. I'd never been a deliberate boy, never would be; but even I had enough sense to know I was acting unsensibly.

Why, then, did I let things proceed? Well, however much I'd played the hell-raiser from earliest schooldays, I'd often likewise shown counterinstincts toward politeness. To this day I retain both these sides of my character, neither a pure virtue nor a pure vice, and each still in periodic, painful contest with the other. In 1966, wedding day approaching, I felt compelling reasons to stop the whole business, even if that meant sabotaging everybody else's plans. But my mannerly disinclination to rock boats prevailed: I stayed the good boy. How, after all, could I break off an arrangement that appeared to gratify my mother so? Hadn't she suffered enough for a spell? Wouldn't I likewise insult the memory of her husband, who'd been similarly fond of my bride-to-be? ("I've known you all your life," he joked to me when I announced our engagement, "and this is the first really *bright* decision I've caught you at.")

Monkeysuits and gowns—all fitted. Preacher, organist, orchestra—all hired. On and on, and no decent way out, I imagined; no time even to decide whether I really wanted a way. And thus, in the confidence of my sublime ignorance, I concluded that I could always divorce if married life didn't work out.

Sixteen years and two children later, my wife and I did part company. Because of that son and that daughter, I will never seriously unwish those years; but they were undeniably hard for me in many respects, and surely more so for my spouse. At length I believed, and still do, that no solution other than divorce would leave us both sane; yet the pain of it overwhelmed me. What hurt, above all, might I bestow as inheritance? The agony of that time lives on in me, though I soon remarried (more happily than anyone deserves), and have remained in a contact with those first children as close and loving as with the three who have followed.

These are thoughts, however odd, that I *do* know I had as I lingered on Stonehouse Mountain this morning, recalling a bubble and a brown fisher. And I thought of how, from an astonishingly young age, I'd vowed to find a region—some beautiful and intriguing country, home to fleet, wild things—and marry it. Thought how I'd courted the wilder parts of Maine, New Hampshire, and Vermont all through my adolescence and then, in my twenties, tied the knot with upper New England.

And I thought, as the poet wrote, of "fallings from us, vanishings."

For a long stretch, I'd remained so in love with this Grafton County that even on the worst day of mudtime my heart would stutter at the simple sight of a certain slope or tree or stream. The stubborn green of an October sidehill surrounded by darkening woods seemed a marvel that all by itself proved life worthwhile. I remember a July moon over Kenyon Hill so apparently near that my first little girl, not yet two at the time, made clutching gestures toward it, imagining candy. I remember my oldest son's wide-eyed, slack-jawed stare at the bank of Trout Brook, from which a January mink had just scampered into nearby jackfirs. I remember the scarlet tanager that came daily out of yellow May woods to a maple by the bedroom where my wife nursed another baby son. I remember that son's little sister, giggling as we cracked the skim-ice on a late March pool with pointy sticks. And now the newest baby goes cross-eyed and furrow-browed as a sulphur butterfly lights on her carriage. In mind it's as if in all seasons the wide, good universe were there for the sake of each child alone.

In recent years, though, my love affair has found itself in trouble. I can no longer take its passions straight, because for every moment of the old exaltation—for every field or moon or mink, every bird or puddle, every blue butterfly or sun-dazed fisher—there comes a grimly compensating recognition. All these glories are under attack as never before.

But have I another divorce in me? And if so, on what grounds? Does one abandon the love of one's life because she's been assaulted? Doesn't one defend her to the death? Here, while so accurate in other respects, the marriage analogy fails. Though I can cherish the lands and waters and animals of a place with a human affection, none will ever *become* human: indeed, that their inner lives remain so irretrievably otherwise is the greater part of their seductiveness to imagination.

But let my puny allegories stand or fall as they will. How little they matter anyhow. I *have* fought as hard as was in me against those luxury "estates" I mentioned earlier, to the extent that on several occasions I've scarcely restrained myself (or been re-strained by others) from physical violence. In company with my wife and friends and neighbors, I have poured cash, time, and fervor into the battle, and as I write our side has happily prevailed. Yet I have also read my *mene, mene, tekel, upharsin.* The town planning board's rejection of a swinish proposal takes note of the dirt-road intersection below us, which the members consider too tricky for such sudden increase in traffic. Nothing noted of the greater, the more obscene peril: that in future deliberations an unencumbered mountainside will be considered not a wondrous treasure but a chunk of real estate.

When things have reached such a turn, "conservation"— however ardently I practice and support it—looks depressingly irrelevant to a stubborn fool like me, because by then something is already past conserving, irretrievably lost. Something spiritual:

once banished, no *genius loci* accepts reinvitation; we're mucking around with eternals here.

For all of that, there will doubtless soon be talk of compromise. (One vociferous—and almost marvelously feather-headed—townsman who spoke all along in the project's favor has lately been elected as a "planner.") Perhaps the developer will settle for seven luxury homes on the wild side of Stonehouse, not fifteen; perhaps he'll put aside a larger segment of his property for conservancy, the one that from the start he has called a park (the very word suggesting the awful diminishment I speak of). Not that my mind will disapprove these enforced concessions, which will be better than nothing. It's only that my heart is an absolutist: mere terms having changed, this stretch of woods and hillside will never again suffice for me and my family.

It's time to go.

※

For a long while, I pledged I'd never inhabit ground I couldn't pee on in broad daylight without worry over observation. Whatever burdens it imposes on her for reasons of gender, my wife has joined in the oath. The day the developer filed his plan with the town, we vowed we'd resist it to the end; but we also put our Stonehouse home on the market and went looking for a bigger spread somewhere else, outside the gentrifying web, affordable. The spot we found sits a good way upriver, and in one respect I should be satisfied for good: with nearly three hundred acres of scrub and ledge to choose from, I'll relieve myself where I damned well please.

Yet my old stipulation, which I once considered a telling metaphor, seems the palest of whimsies now. Even after we discovered the new site—full of game and cedar swamp, bordered by granite palisade, barely dotted by a bungalow and workshop—I recognized for my own part that our move could at best be a holding action. One can piss his bladder out on the earth and still be shriven of all that really matters. The breadth and situation of the place will ensure privacy, but this isn't what we're after. It is not only that both my wife and I relish the human connectedness of a true community, the kind of community that so-called development does much to sunder; it's also that if we reach the point of valuing privacy over other qualities, we will have admitted defeat, will have bought a mere illusion. If ours becomes the last domain of apparent wildness in the country or state, then we'll live in a park ourselves, as artificial as some millionaire's fenced-in preserve or that biospheric bubble one lately reads of. We may not see another soul from where we live, but as I say, the very air will have changed.

What on earth can I want, then? I ask the same of myself, to the point of hysteria; and in answering I sometimes recall the title of a poem by an unlikely hero, insurance executive Wallace Stevens: "The Pleasures of Merely circulating." Or I summon the closing passage of yet another of his poems, "Esthétique du mal":

> And out of what one sees and hears and out
> Of what one feels, who could have thought to make
> So many selves, so many sensuous worlds,
> As if the air, the midday air, was swarming
> With the metaphysical changes that occur,
> Merely in living as and where we live.

I want to live where a meeting with a brown-phase fisher is never a commonplace, but always a *possibility*. I would a hundred times prefer to encounter that creature on home ground than travel to Kenya or wherever to behold a basking leopard. Tourism won't do: to thrill at that leopard, I'd have to inhabit his landscape. I'd rather wander a path across the very landscape I dwell in, certain that by such mere circulation, however stealthily undertaken, I might slip among its secretive, metaphysical wonders, as I've done for so much of my life.

Where on the planet can such country lie anymore? That, of course, is the rub. The leopard's every move has been charted by the organizers of the photographic safari; the guests will not fail to snap him from their Land Rovers. Amazing, then, that I recall dim markings on maps of Africa, representing—we were told— places untrod by human feet. Though our teachers betrayed, needless to say, their Eurocentric notions of humanity, notions whose political implications still prove enormous, I—as a child of European extraction myself—must admit my childhood enchantment with these obtuse descriptions. As a grownup I wince to know that someone may have fitted the big cat with a radio transmitter, kin to the cassette players in the native villages where young men pass in knock-off Michael Jordan basketball shoes. So much for what we called darkest Africa, whose very undarkening, whose whitening, fits my mood of disaster.

More locally, how staggering to read New Englander Ralph Waldo Emerson's claim of a bare hundred and sixty years ago— less than twice the span of his own rich lifetime—that "*Nature,* in the common sense, refers to essences unchanged by man; space, the air, the river, the leaf."

Fifteen luxury estates on Stonehouse Mountain.

From the White Mountains to the Black Forest, foliage shriveling in its acid bath.

The "blue Danube," so thick you can almost walk across it.

The crew of the spaceship Atlantis—one member no doubt on watch for orbiting junk—beams congratulations to *Star Wars* producer George Lucas at the goddamned Academy Award ceremonies.

For me such bad news underlies even a fair amount of good news: for example, that the frightening hole our ingenuity has rent in the ozone layer can perhaps be patched up by the same ingenuity. Logic requires me to rejoice at such a prospect, but I claim no logic for my feelings: should human nature repair what it has wrought in nonhuman, there will no longer *be* such a thing as the nonhuman. The heavens themselves are park enough as it is. That moon's no magical candy for a daughter, even in my fancy. And though she and her sisters and brothers have all been keen for evening hikes to high prominences, they've never looked on stars that kindled in a truly unknown realm. I feel almost cursed to have been so blessed myself as a child.

And yes, how stubborn old blessing has made me! On the day that a rocket flew up to probe Venus, two grouse flew up ahead of my great bitch Bessie. Don't ask me to name that rocket nor say what of use its crew brought home; but until I die I'll remember each inch of the joyously arduous trek up the maple-crazy slope above Pony Hill, and Bessie's point on that double.

"Does No One at All Ever Feel This Way in the Least?" asked Robert Frost in a poem so entitled, one already quaint by 1952. And quainter still, I answer him yes:

> And now, O sea, you're lost by aeroplane.
> Our sailors ride a bullet for a boat.
> Our coverage of distance is so facile
> It makes us to have had a sea in vain.
> Our moat around us is no more a moat,
> Our continent no more a moated castle.

I know the argument—to which, again, I can offer no logical counter—that it's as much a "natural" thing for human speculation and endeavor to keep broadening themselves as it is for my fisher to root a hare from under some fallen hemlock, or for me to fire on a pair of game birds; and that the 747 has its roots in the warrior's chariot—not to mention that my precision-made Winchester looks back on his pike. Perhaps some son or daughter will delight, as many people obviously must, in a naturalism so conceived. I recognize here that I speak, as one tends to do, of things that have charged my *own* imaginative life, things whose alteration feels like painful, personal attack, and whose disappearance bodes a death.

So mortally wounded, I come back and back to the same painful stand: What father am I? What vision do I leave behind?

༄

It may sound as though my restlessness were new, and my younger love for this north country the emotion of a naive boy. But my only genuine naiveté lay in a radical underestimation of the *speed* with which today's remote New England corner—let alone those dark African map-splotches—would become tomorrow's suburb or resort. Although I began to dream of Idaho when the very first fern bar opened in the nearest town of size, it was a bit as I'd dreamed of divorce even as I married for the first time: my innocence, as I say, was to feel no immediate urgency in either speculation.

I had spent a good deal of time in the west, and had loved

every minute; yet there existed something deep within me that clove to the density, the greenery, the variety of the woods and even of the much maligned weather in the upper Northeast. What could be more beautiful than the Yellowstone reaches of Montana, the Green River valley in Utah, the Wind River Mountains in Wyoming, the Sangre de Cristos in New Mexico, the Maroon Bells of Colorado? But I remained no more than a rapt visitor among these intoxications, and while I got a kick out of cowboys, I identified, however presumptuously, with backland Yankees.

I did recognize, for all of this, one powerful advantage the Western mountain states held over my beloved trio of Maine, New Hampshire, and Vermont. They were, so to say, a little closer to dark old Africa. That is, even if they were equally prey to the international conspiracy against beauty and wonder (indeed, perhaps more so: once, seeing a Wyoming strip mine, I imagined my damnation in advance), those states beyond the Mississippi had *size*. If a pustule like Aspen popped up and festered, that still left a hell of a lot of Colorado; so did Rocky Flats. For every Jackson Hole and every wretched mineral operation, there existed a hundred barely populated hamlets to east or south or north. Once the cake got frosted near Santa Fe, you could trek back into mountains that made our own look live loaves on a shelf.

And since I'd for some reason never been to Idaho, nor ever heard it much spoken of by exactly the wrong people, it became a new place in mind. Vague, latent.

That Idaho.

※

I finally visited the state late last summer, and at least where I roamed, it looked all the Idaho it ever could. I found things that have long bound me to the East—forests, chiefly, and none restricted like many Western stands to single species—combined with a superb, non-Eastern vastness. I even came on a stretch of river that would serve: not blue-ribbon stuff, but its trout being wild it was good enough, in part precisely for being yet undiscovered by the blue-ribbon crowd in their spanking Orvis duds. Though all my reserves had been poured into the new property back home, I did discover a modest riverside farm for sale at a beggar's price. Someday, maybe, I thought—before it's too late.

It was too late already. Not long after getting home, my brain crowded with fantasies which I believed I'd sobered out of, I read the inevitable, crushing article in one of my conservation magazines. There was furor in good quarters over a proposed development (what a word! as if God had left the job undone) on the fabulous Snake River. The golf course; the jetboat marina; the complex of condominums with 24-hour security. This horror will quite likely fail to go through, but there will be another compromise, and, for all its hard effects on my soul, something in my blood—the very blood I've passed on to five children—will not be compromised.

And yet it must.

※

I look out the window of a house laid bare: high on Stonehouse Mountain, where the foliage comes late, the scrawny hardwoods have just started to show their meek pastels, which they seem to pull back into themselves whenever a cloud sails over. In our driveway my truck cringes under its burden of furniture, books, dog crates, crockery, firearms. Orts and fragments.

Suddenly I recall one more walk, with my fourth child Catherine in the venerable riding pack. It was the sort of languid August midday when the woods go silent as a cave, so that the little girl's voice seemed to fill the countryside. *Yesterday,* she sang, *all my troubles seemed so far away./ Now it looks as though they're here to stay./ Oh, I believe in yesterday.* She was three years old, and the song but a song; yet I needed to labor some against my own tears, her tune ringing truer than she could yet know.

Within my lifetime no jetboat will roil the waters beside the farm I found in Idaho. But once my children live there, they'll hear such a snarl in their own—the *tock* of the clubbed ball, the growl of the patrolling Rottweiler. I whistle for the blonde son and daughter who want to ride north with me in the truck; I sigh and try to feel practical, since I know what I know: as well to move our paltry twenty-five New England miles as to wrench up stakes more radically.

There seems wrench enough, after all, in leaving one more local town where once we dreamed of permanence, where a handful of friends and a handful of wilds will remain. The prospect of hunting up their replacements elsewhere seems sufficiently daunting too. Inner lives, both human and natural, will reveal themselves at a slow pace; that's the rural New England manner. Yet the greater ache is that those lives, like the ones we abandon today, may prove as fragile as our boy's one bold and bright expression, a few short hours past, up there at height-of-land.

III

Presences

Hushed plane, the pond.
Men hug their whiskey
whiffs of bait,

Laconic chat:
or God damn this,
but ordinary.

one to another;
his door (like an oven's,
"Doin' some good?"

"Blackfly" will call
will rally from silence
It's half past ten.

others stay through
the small smelt bite.
What of Ben,

He sniffs and blows,
some part of their bodies
a shout all worthless,

with platitude,
not even longing . . .
and situation

with a hopeful season,
to start anew.
in the utter chill

visionary
The dullness is pure.
except it be

Ice-fishers' lights.
jugs inside
potbelly smoke,

an idle joke;
although such words
Snowmobile roads

now and then,
infernal within)
Or dirty Duane,

words much the same
a moment or two,
Blackfly and Lou

the darkness till dawn,
What *of* this town,
who's outside skimming

thinks vaguely of women,
out loud across
directionless,

devoid of embrace,
at least for sex.
much at odds,

season of gods,
Outside, the flags
are utterly slack,

prey down under
No signs, no wonders,
the care with which

Still little city.
as they loiter among
sock-wool and sweat.

or God damn that
aren't even angry
thread our shacks

Big Lou throws open
and cries to a neighbor,
the one we call

and the neighborhood
then sink back in.
and all the quietened

whether or not
this bobhouse crew?
his ice-hole's o's?

and thinks to name
the frozen surface:
a shout all shoddy

containing nothing,
Just part of a mood
it might be imagined,

of resolution
on their planted poles
betraying no

to clasp their lures.
no mystery . . .
all night men linger,

as if in prayer
by which to address
part of what holds us

amid this fetor
a sense that early,
our flags will all

Epiphany
a yodel of steam!
in this merest of towns,

of light seem bored.
city, how still,
go by above,

for a novel fish,
some thing they're feeling.
under crude ceilings

with speechless friends.
before the dawn
at once, together,

–o bright palaver!
So runs our fancy
although our shanties'

O little city,
how still we see thee.
even here,

embrace the year.

or a novel way
Surely this is
beaded with pitch,

Surely, surely
(or sooner, or later)
tremble and shimmy.

o every hole
in the absence of sound
very beams

we think, it's cold;
Still, the stars
and still may love

A Track

HERE I RECALL a story I heard from a certain Henry, who—along with other, more improvisatory callings—worked as a woodsman and guide until his death at 82, two decades back. I use my own language, however, hoping to avoid the awkwardness of dialect writing, and more importantly to avoid the least hint of burlesquing or poking fun at my old friend. Not that Henry was a somber man. When he chose, in fact, he could be among the funniest humans I've met. It's just that this particular narrative's intentions were scarcely comic.

Or so I say, to this day uncertain what its real motives were. I can't even decide whether Henry meant it for literal truth, partial truth, or pure fiction. Like anyone's recollections, perhaps it melded all of these. Whatever the case, the story struck at something inside me, something that may itself have been more or less invented. I may, that is, have forced Henry's facts—as I'll call them for convenience—into an order they never possessed. And yet I persist, having known the teller so very well.

I could say that I read Henry like a book.

🦡

Early one morning, gone outdoors to check on his hunting dogs, my friend came on disaster. Kneeling by the kennel, he studied the long track in mud beside it, a hoofish mark that he likened to a stretched Valentine's heart, the cleft on top pinched narrow. The print's delicacy surprised Henry, since whatever made it possessed such obvious power: the fence's bullwire had been ripped like cloth, and the head of his setter bitch crushed almost flat, dark blood freezing on the gravel. The other dogs, one young hound and one veteran, whimpered and balked as he coaxed them from their nailkeg houses.

Now in those days the local citizenry found itself divided—in more than one sense—between farmers on this hand and, on that, people who lived mostly by logging or trapping or hunting or, like Henry himself, some combination of the three. Today, the farms gone and timber operations more and more mechanized, the breach is between oldtime natives in general and newcomers, who have small knowledge of regional histories and habits.

But that is a different tale altogether.

Henry referred to farmers—no matter what kind—as Tater Pluckers. Though they often seemed to amuse him, he found them irritating too, especially for their tendency to exaggerate ordinary adversity, to see in a heavy thunderstorm the omen of flood or in the odd dead shoat a coming epidemic. A few mornings prior to his bird dog's death, some wild thing had gutted a few sheep and ripped through a flock of pondfowl near the village, and had therefore in the tater-plucking imagination immediately become a bear or wolf . . . which the farm folk would hope to kill as quickly as possible in the interest of their clumsy tame beasts and stock-still crops. Henry therefore pledged to himself not to mention the marauding of his kennel. He loved a tall tale himself, but only as entertainment, not as a presention of reality.

Of course there lay a kind of bigotry in Henry's attitude, even if the attitude had some validation in fact. I myself have noticed how the intrusion of the genuinely novel or unexpected causes farm myths to grow like weeds: yarns about hay wagons overturned in the night; about some child fright-frozen by a thing so big she couldn't see her father's barn behind it; about horses flung over the pasture walls; about windows torn brutally from their casings, ravenous cold air rushing through the gaps. Each may contain the germ of truth and none be true.

The tater plucker and a fellow like Henry might be distinguished from one another in a hundred ways, but most clearly by their responses to the wondrous. And yet Henry depended like everyone—if in slighter measure—on the farmers' very obsessions, which were increasingly becoming those of humans in general. Even there, in the far north, one noticed people's ever greater lust for efficiency, their ever greater attachment to the predictable.

Thus, while Henry's came closer than anyone else's to an ideally independent life, even he could disappoint. Electricity reached his township in 1953, for instance, and although he waited four years, he finally installed not only lighting but also—more communal modes of entertainment obviously dead—a television. It depressed me profoundly to hear him laugh at the stupid TV comedies, since on his worst day he could be so much more witty himself.

In short, as Henry proved honest enough to recognize, there were flaws in his own mythology. Or at least, sharing those flaws, I myself feel duty-bound to acknowledge them.

Yet how can any of us survive in a world whose every meaning is equivocal, in which no categorical opinion can bear scrutiny? We cannot. And so we persist in our convictions, which are really no more than intuition; we persist in a sort of faith—that our visions of the world will at length be purged of contradiction, that we're neither mere fabulists nor hypocrites.

I persisted and persist in imagining a different and better figure inside Henry, one who exchanged greeting over the centuries with a fellow concerned to chip rough flint to a point. I felt, and still do, that a predator sees things that others don't. And right through his old age Henry remained among the best hunters I would ever know.

Like even the most skilled predator, of course, he was unevenly lucky. But who would want his luck guaranteed? So he asked me once, after I'd spent a few fruitless days of deer stalking with him. Without a long wait for it, he reminded me, I wouldn't properly prize the hunter's best moment: when his sense of landscape, his prey's rush, and the swing of his weapon all come together. Like grace to me, such an instant, redeeming the many others in which the most rudimentary lessons of my past have seemed useless, the countryside alien and jumbled, the game apparently extinct, a gun no better than a club.

☙

Henry told how he gathered up the body of his dead setter and
lugged it to the barren well uphill, where in successive layers of
clay several other dogs already mouldered, most gone by natural
causes. I'll guess that the November air produced in him a tart
nausea—nostalgia, to name it too simply—and that he spoke
aloud the dogs' several names, each word issuing as a breath-
cloud, then dispersing itself, almost at once.

There were, he said, the usual frustrations and enchantments
of planning. Skipping breakfast, Henry went down to his shop,
to that companionable clutter of boots, ropehanks, blankets,
deerhorns, ax-heads, rifles and scatterguns on pins. What gear
would he need? Astride an old stool (I own it now), he kept
getting ahead of himself, cramming one thing after another into a
rucksack till it nearly burst, fetching the stuff out again and
starting over too quickly, anxious simply to *go*.

I fancy Henry's son stepping into the shop and, sensing wel-
come, letting go a string of questions. What happened to the dog?
Why don't you know? What will you do? Where are you heading?
After a few minutes Henry's wife comes in too. Shocked as she
may be by the setter's death, at length she shows a near-smile of
indulgence and patience, aware that something more than grief or
rage has robbed her husband's appetite.

☙

Henry would outlive both wife and son by decades, for they'd be
killed together in an automobile accident. There was another
child as well, a much older daughter. She must still be alive,
though no one has seen her for an age: unlike her small sister,
born later along, she did not even attend the double funeral. But
all this makes another story too. Or stories.

☙

Henry set off at noon in a long line west, partly as he said for the
plain sake of climbing Binder's Ridge, so steeply pitched he had to
pull himself upward by rocky outcroppings.

I picture all this also: Henry pausing halfway as a cloud slides briskly downhill; he watches his hand, arm, and torso turn color as the pale sun dims. A flake or two falls by. White-shod, a hare flushes off to one side. In front of his nose Henry sees an owl's hairball; he knocks it on granite, tumbling tiny bones, one of which he secures in his pocket, talisman of the kind he likes to carry.

At height-of-land, he headed slightly north of west, into the wind. The squall came on, but he walked easily along the rim. It was cropped and trampled by wild browsers, so that Henry scolded himself: no gun, the deer season winding down, food hard to come by through a winter unless you dickered with a tater plucker. He stooped to a brook, which tasted of softwood, and therefore, I'd bet, of afternoons with certain dead woodsmen he thanked God he'd known alive. He must have spoken their calling names as he had the dogs'. Gus. Bill. Warren. Carter. He must have been tempted to go back for his rifle, to give up this weirder stalk for a more practical. And yet those same names may have urged him on to whatever this was he was doing.

After several hours, Henry decided on the quick, cross-lots drop back to his house. He told me he ran the clearings and swung through second growth like a kid. Shuffling his feet in the final meadow, he left a trail like the ones the farmers kept reporting: great dragging strides that plowed the frozen dew and new snow, two obtuse lines of V's.

He winked at me as he remembered this, since he knew the real track to be delicate, even dainty.

※

Henry's own track would mar the woodsfloor for nearly two months before he finally picked up a skein of the Valentines—the odd one clear, the others wetted out—on the Agate Town road. He followed to a slue between two hills, then lost them in the slush of the bog.

That night, there was conversation after the son had been put to bed.

"Should we worry for him?" Henry's wife asked.

"The boy? I don't think so. I'm surprised the thing came as

close as Agate Hill, never mind the dogpen." Together, they dismissed the tales of peril in town, resolving still to say nothing about the kennel killing until something could be known. His wife's name was Faith. She and Henry were well suited one to the other.

❦

On the 6th of January, Henry was camped by the same bog. Recalling that night for me, he said he'd felt tired and fractious from having carried his grip through a gluey snow: bedding, tarpaulin, sealed-beam headlight mounted on a board and, worst of all, its twelve-volt battery. Dark came so early that he was bored by seven o'clock, uncomfortable and contemptuous. He began to ponder all that had passed since the bitch's death. Was it some obscure lust for revenge that led him here, or was it in fact a trail? Or was it both, and more?

Suddenly the night sounds—the nattering of pine spills on his tarp, the far lamentations of an owl, of which he hadn't quite been conscious before—stopped. The wind died, the hemlock stood unwaving.

He reported that next day he was sure he'd been looked at. Ranging gingerly around the heath, he came on a mammoth windfall, under which the ground was cuffed clear of snow and twigs: a resting place, now abandoned, with a string of heart-shaped prints leading to it, another neatly away. Kneeling, Henry told me, he caught a faint whiff like that of an herb whose name he could not summon.

The outgoing tracks led further around the bog until, directly opposite his camp, they turned as if to cross the muddle of slush, water and tussock. At that turning stood a small crowd of up-rooted bushes and saplings, curiously piled so that in silhouette they looked like a wigwam. This odd cairn aroused in him, Henry said, a bizarre fear, not entirely unpleasant.

There was no getting over the slue. He continued to the south, following its trickle downhill. The tracks did not re-emerge, yet on circling back and walking the campsite side, he did not find them either. He wrapped his provisions in the tarpaulin and pulleyed them into a tree, all but the battery, which he'd take home against the cold. It might already need charging. (I smirk at myself to recollect such a particular: how would my hunter-gatherer have reacted to the mysterious process in Miller's garage, blued terminals sucking in odd nurture?)

※

On the following day, Henry waited till dusk before setting out for camp again. A certain smell suggested a seasonal storm in the making, so that on reaching the tent he whacked down evergreen boughs for more bedding. I envision chickadees flicking out of the trees like motes from a beaten rug, runnels of ground rodents, so recently uncovered by the thaw, fading under powder, and Henry both stirred to think of these creatures's numbers and sobered by how puny they are—the tiny bird, the mouse, the vole. Then he is stirred again by the contrasting thought of this thing he seeks, so singular, maybe dangerous.

That second night proved less tedious than the first. Henry could hear the skim-ice stiffening; the stubborn fall of snow intrigued him, made the evening pass like reverie, both slow and chaotic. Several times he nodded. By midnight the snow reached nearly to his tree-hung tarp, which he went out and punched, so that the weight of the storm would not sag or break it.

He must ultimately have dropped into heavier slumber, for he spoke of a dryness in his throat after he was awakened by a sound, muffled by the risen drifts: an odd click, punctuated by loud slaps, as on bare skin. Quietly, he pushed a peephole through the bank at the head of his shelter, then felt for the leads from battery to light. He reached with cold, sleep-crippled fingers for the eye-glasses he'd stored in a boot, put them on, and touched a loose wire to a terminal.

Could that have been the sheen of an almost hairless flank, thewed with the long muscles of fleet things? His glasses had frosted, he told me, so he wasn't sure. He rubbed the lenses with a shirt tail, he blinked, he squinted. This time, nothing. He swung the headlight. Nothing. Snow fell through the lamp-beam, and he caught himself some while later, lost in a trance, watching the flakes drift noiselessly earthward.

I've been lost that way myself more than once.

At dawn Henry clambered from his tent, snowshoeing on a line to the sighting, such as it was. Nothing. The snow had gone on falling all night. He began another circuit of the slough, not certain whether the ice had sufficiently thickened to walk it. He digressed in his story to say how once, on snowshoes, he'd broken through a springhole, to speak of the agony in his feet and calves, of the struggle to disengage from his bindings, of the long hike home, ice beaded up to his buttocks so that he had to hold himself apart as he trudged.

He couldn't tell whether certain blurred lines in the snow marked the creature's going or were mere windrows made by storm. He could not find the deadfall he'd discovered two evenings before; each hump he kicked free of snow turned out to be wrong. He screeched in anger at two innocent, paper-white rabbits that bolted crazily out of one of them. And he screeched inwardly as well: when will you learn to *see*, to *notice*?

Henry of all people—who noticed more in a week than I in a lifetime, who seemed to see *everything*—berated himself that way.

He found at least the wigwam. One trail, or windrow, led away from it, sheer up a ledge to the east. Three times his snowshoes failed their purchase just short of the brow, and he slid, arms swinging wildly for balance, back down. Once a sharp twinge whipped like electricity from shoulder to sternum, prompting a brief hypochondriac fantasy and a defeatist thought: home! home! home! But persisting, he made the top, where a snow-dusted puddle in the granite held a heart's shape. Next to that mark, a cairn of vegetation, juniper tuft and winter-purpled hardhack. It was smaller than the first one.

All imaginable trails away from this spot died quickly into utter vagueness. When at last he quit for the day, Henry saw that he'd tracked a giant fowl's foot on the landscape, the Valentine its spur. He skidded the ledge to camp, got all his grip, and moved back houseward.

❦

In the spruce little farms downcountry, paranoia bloomed like a crop whose season was winter: folks laid Ralph Hicks's death, for example, at the generous age of ninety, to some awful confrontation behind his silo; and if no tracks showed there beside those of free-ranging poultry, then the creature must have come, if not on wings, through air nonetheless—how else could it have thrown Ralph's collie, tethered in the loft of the locked barn, through the upstairs door, so that they found her next morning swinging like the angel Death over her poor owner's rigid corpse?

🦋

It was now the middle of February, the land's contours lit by inchoate hardwood buds, lustrous even in afternoon's lengthening shadows, which vanished in the frequent squalls but reappeared as suddenly. Henry's own family began to doubt him, and he himself. Who might serve as a witness? He settled on his friend Edward, a retired railroad man, but woods-wise.

The companions set out at two, and by late afternoon it seemed that fine weather had established itself, Macky Mountain briefly taking the color of honey, then darkening. That night, rapt in conversation inside the tent, the two men would scarcely notice the return of snow. And Henry alone noticed— or did he?—that silence, that lapse of wind, and again that irrepressible idea of being *observed*. His groping headlight startled Edward, then seemed to amuse him, for it showed only those ambiguous depressions, probably windrows again, now blanking in the storm.

Come morning, Henry walked the bog with his friend and pointed out the first cairn to him. Edward said nothing till, led to the top of the easterly ledge, he saw the second, which now looked fabricated, even to Henry—childish somehow, pitiably small.

"What are you trying to prove?"

Henry ignored a certain thrust in Edward's question: "I want to get an eye on it."

"Kill it?"

"Maybe if it rips up another one of my dogs. But not even then, probably. . . ."

❧

You could say that Henry abandoned his project, and that he never did. At all events, he did not again take up the actual, the literal track.

The mudtime passes quickly into somnolent summer, unproductive torpor, fruits of a loosely controlled but contentful boredom. Henry daps for sunfish with his boy, jigs on his knee the third child, the surprise, the new baby girl, all appetite and greedy fingers. His wife grows plump and lovely.

I imagine it all.

There has yet been no crisis, of any kind.

A family of raccoons grows up and scatters from the dead elm by Henry's porch. Hosts of salamanders prick the pond, and frogs twang like banjos. The woods go dry as cotton, undergrowth so dense and copperhead flies so thick and vicious that Henry loiters near home, becoming slightly slack in the belly.

A great lull in the town mythology has followed the loss, predictably construed as abnormal, of a few spring lambs and one calf. Working their immense warm-weather hours, the farmers trade fewer tales: anecdotes, rather, clipped by the heat and flattened out by the men's weariness from a contest with vegetable relentlessness—the flock of skunks, and how they stank when the sicklebar dismembered them; new modes of outwitting corn-thieving crows; the unhappy turn in a local girl's reputation; so on.

By this time the silos broadcast their heavy stench. The hills recede into haze. On odd nights, though, the air clears, and a significant wind—from just north of west—winnows the clouds from Macky Mountain and, October-like, the stars are sharp. Henry feels then a surge in his lower torso, a shame at his softened body. The kennel fills with drifts of summer hair. He pledges soon to cut the dogs' feed and his own, for soon grouse will explode from apple and aspen, amorous bucks paw the redolent turf, the fur of the fox turn prime. There will be the dazzling energy of wild duck-flight, and beavers pounding the river as he makes his way before dawn to a blind.

His son now and then catches him in an empty stare, asks his thoughts. Were fate always kind, the boy might one day have found their measure—as I hope to have done myself.

For it seems to me, as it must have to Henry, that the heart-shaped presence has always been at hand, that no one among us will understand nor give up the effort to understand it.

I imagine that winter's memories—the slaps, the mysterious cairns, the spicy scent under the empty windfall—mixing with recalls of autumn clouds, sudden on a gamey sidehill, the dog unaccountably raising its hackles, deep silence, a nervous thrill in the stomach.

Yes, his poor son might eventually have felt all this. I know that I have felt it, in part for hearing Henry's unfinished tale, and in part because it *was* unfinished.

❦

Let us imagine Henry's thoughts when, some summer day, he looks far down into the valley at a smoking combine, which creeps through a field behind a pigeon-toed tractor, the gold of grain-stalks ceding to geometries.

It is as if the farmer's ceaseless efforts to uncover ground might lead him to some knowledge, fixed, eternal, beyond transforming.

Tutto nuovo

S OON THE GRAPEVINES would bloom—subtle, precipitous, here and gone. Already the broom's flowers were just shy of full yellow. Depending on the resolve or dither of the winds, grasses bent in unison or flurried in contradiction, bright poppies attending, though somehow these looked both good-natured and bemused, like tourists aping a native behavior. In the gusts' lulls, the strength of the sun was a surprise. Green lizards emerged then to lounge on the masonry, pulses in their throats the only signs of how alert they remained.

This was not of course home ground but the Chianti, where—thanks to the Guggenheim family—four years ago my own family spent much of the spring and half the summer.

April's days would generally turn blustery and spit rain. Yet Beppina, our nearest neighbor, greeted me buoyantly in all weathers: "Ciao, amico! Che bella giornata!" She'd aspirate the hard *c* in the word for friend, a sound characteristic of the Tuscan countryfolk . . . and the Moors from whom centuries back they borrowed it.

The Arabism of Beppina's salute suggested how little her community discards. Slowly acquired, a phonic mannerism lingers. Or—another detail that compelled me for private reasons—a cut oak is used to the tip of its least twig: on these hills there was none of the slash I'd left behind on the mountain across from my house, which the loggers were jobbing; neat faggots of kindling instead, each bound by a pliant branch from the parent tree, lay in the dooryards.

It goes without saying that all kitchen- and barn-waste returns to the soil there.

Such a place seemed "conservative" in a way that the then incumbent Ronald Reagan would never have understood. The unfettered entrepreneurism he championed (even calling it magic) could at all events never *literally* conserve in the manner of Beppina's community. How many of his constituents, myself included, might say with her for instance that theirs was the same neighborhood as their great-great-grandmother's? Beppina had a new washing machine, and her husband a toy-sized Fiat, but she conducted her life much as her ancestress had. Though two of her four children still lived under her roof, they were grown men and women, so Beppina had turned with greater dedication than ever to her livestock—ducks, pigs, rabbits, pigs, pigeons—and her beloved olive trees. However we judge this style, it's surely far different from the volatile one of American capitalism, in which novelty seems a shibboleth.

But I must distinguish between novelty and newness. Though those mornings were raw, Beppina would chirp, "Tutto nuovo, il mondo!" By which she likely meant that, no matter the chill, winter's back was broken, spring couldn't help arriving. If the mist made us shiver, through it we saw the roses, espaliered against her hogyard wall, creeping toward full color; cuckoos jabbered from the thickets; the ducks and pigeons were sitting on eggs; bean-stems made little arcs along her garden's surface.

Beppina neither described nor desired a slate wiped clean: everything *was* all new, but in that place it was palpably ancient as well.

※

I hope not to sound like the naif who's charmed—especially in hindsight—by an unfamiliar quaintness, who too easily applauds the manners of his foreign hosts while denigrating his own people and place. I know, for instance, that if the Tuscan peasant's life has followed a steady pattern for generations, this is in large measure because the landowner's has done the same.

❧

Once arrived at our rented house, I'd naturally scrutinized the local wildlife—or, given the Italian love of food in all guises, its absence. (In this respect, that conservative impulse is less robust: curbs on taking songbirds, say, are widely flouted.) Once and not again, I saw the spoor of a fox in the vineyard downhill. At another point I thought I'd discovered a tiny deer track, but it turned out on inspection to be a roving goat's. I did hear the shouts of cock pheasants, even after dark, the lusts of spring so general.

Some admire the pheasant, that Oriental who thrives all over the world, even or especially where the native game has more or less vanished; but to me the bird's a disappointment. I'm too conscious of him as an import, and thus somehow a phony. (Please don't remind me of my lifelong allegiance to the German brown trout.) Even a naturally bred pheasant, even a canny survivor of many attempts on his life, strikes me as a glorified barnyard creature, as happy behind wire mesh as he'd be in the wild. Given what I admit is my prejudice, I don't even care for his appearance, highly praised in some quarters. I find it garish. I can't help but contrast it to that of the gamebird I chase back home: the handsomeness of a ruffed grouse consists to some extent in its having forever been part of its own landscape.

These digressions suggest the mixed responses I still have to our Italian sojourn. Immensely drawn to the local conservatism, I seemed also New World enough to balk at how *domestication* (not to mention the class system) sustained it.

But I must resist the appeal of facile dialectic: America/Europe. Which might subsume Young/Old, Hunter/Agrarian, Domestic/Wild, and so on. Things are never so neat, least of all my own moods.

❧

When I was much younger I spent a lot of time in Europe. Bumming. Studying. Working. Languages came to me without much strain, and I had a smug, erroneous, image of myself as cosmopolite, for all that I was in my teens and early twenties.

I missed hunting over there, though. I couldn't help it.

For most European hunters are essentially mere agents of the kill, and thus more accurately called *shooters.* Deep knowledge of game, terrain and dog is left to the servant classes, who must contrive to scare a live target into the shooter's presence. It's all really a kind of safariing, and not for me. When I hunt, I mean to do the important stuff myself.

So I sensed before too long that "cosmopolitanism" would exact a price I couldn't pay, the abandonment of all I understood as true hunting. At about 27, therefore, I looked on my European days as things of the past and, with a wild, typically youthful shift in convictions, became a sort of nativist.

I was making my living by then as a rookie Ivy League pro-fessor, surrounded by folks who knelt before capital E-C Eu-ropean Culture. (Such adulation itself seems quaint in an era grown sentimentally attached to chronicling that culture's mal-feasances.) Among mini-T. S. Eliots and puppy Popes, I took Whitman—along with Robert Johnson, Louis Armstrong, and others—for my bard, barbaric yawp for my idiom, the open collar for my look. Any ventures away from the woods and waters of the wilder northeast would be selective and rare: to decoy mid-Atlantic geese; to put my dogs on southern quail; to float a fly over big western trout.

I applauded what I took to be the average American's reaction to rank, which, if not hostile, still refused the automatic deference that Old World gentry seemed to expect as birthright. It pleased me that in the small New Hampshire town where I lived blood sports belonged primarily to the laboring classes. And it pleased me further that, despite my fancy Ph.D., my best teachers had been . . . what? Well, if the word meant only "country person," as it does in much of the world, I'd call them peasants. They taught me about trout, bass, and salmon, about deer and hare, woodcock and grouse, pointer and hound, tree and stream.

❦

My twenties were given to a bogus *politesse,* my thirties to an only slightly less affected barbarism, but in that Chianti spring and summer I was perhaps in a quintessentially middle-aged year: the forty-fifth. Middleness. Marginality. Never did I sense these more strongly than in those fields near Siena. Could I lay claim to nothing besides simplism and banality—it was "nice" being there, I missed America—and did even such platitude strand me in contradiction?

Daily, I rose to run for an hour. Passing goat-shouldered men and women at work among furrows and vines, I felt a little frivolous, but I meant to be ready for the following fall. My kind of hunting has always been physically demanding, and I'm driven to keep it so, an obsession that's itself a bit "American." Maybe.

After my runs, I'd write. Oddly, though, I was *less* obsessive than at home about that dimension of my life. There seemed more time in Italy; or perhaps, my perspective altered, I felt that time needn't be measured exclusively by accomplishment; or, most accurately, I remembered that a sense of accomplishment could accompany all manner of action: propping our eight-week-old so that she could study (her expression deserved the verb) a hearth-fire; stalking lizards with her four-year-old brother; slowly experiencing a supper that had begun with the morning's trip to the open market at Sinalunga, where we compared these tomatoes to those and those; beholding the Chianti evening's arrival, its very shadows multihued.

Granted, ours was a kind of paid vacation, nothing workaday about it. Still, I was stunned to discover how many quotidian pleasures there were in this foreign business called civilization. It offered so much *courtesy*, to borrow a Castiglionian resonance. Why had it taken me till now to encounter all this again—or, more honestly, for the first time?

On the other hand, how I longed to lie outdoors by my hunting camp, ancient transistor tuned to baseball. I'd sigh for it, inwardly hearing the crackle and whine, the frequent override from Quebec, the crescendo of the static. (Or was it fan applause? What had *happened*?) Behind the outhouse, owls would be calling back and forth till it seemed the woods were dense with tuneful dogs.

Damn those cock pheasants, squawking into the night! I'd listen to them and wonder whether the woodcock were just then towering over the Beeson pasture and the village ballfield, and in what numbers. I missed blundering onto a brood of grouse on a June sidehill, missed the subsequent broken-wing act of the hen.

Oh, it was good to be in the Chianti, right enough, to be away from those grouse and those woodcock, from the broadwing hawk, the whitetail, the fisher, deft spirits who—visibly or not—always inhabit the quickest part of my poems. For I imagined such absence might allow me to revise those poems in a new, objective way. Far from home ground, from my unbookish hunting partners on one hand and encroaching, greedy developers on the other, I might put a little more polish into the verse. A little less yawp, a little more *dulce et utile*.

I'd brought along the entire Divine Comedy, on the sophomoric premise that Dantean cultivation would more easily rub off on me as I reencountered the master more or less on his own turf. By mid-June, needless to say, I hadn't seen a single stanza. Instead, I was devouring Roger Angell's wondrous baseball book, *Season Ticket,* each of its essays a pleasure to consider in a spot to which its subject matter was irrelevant.

But no, not irrelevant at all:

> There's nothing new here; there's no end to this, year after year,
> and yet each time out, each spring, it feels surprising as well as
> comforting, utterly fresh and known by heart.

That passage shook me when I read it, and not by its elegance alone. Like any excellent writer, irrespective of subject, Angell dazzled as well by his accuracy of observation, which in this case went serendipitously to the heart of my own crude Italian musings. I was wrong as ever to construe life's choices as intensity, striving, "freshness" versus contemplation, cultivation, "tradition" —or, more abstractly, America versus Europe. A career should tend to inclusion, not antimony: to thoughts, feelings and gestures that surprise, as Angell has it, even as they comfort.

※

One morning I interrupted my run to hide behind a generous bush of *ginestrone*. From there I spied on Beppina, as if I might discover the secret of her spirit. She was fussing over the olive trees, originally planted, I think, by her great-grandfather-in-law. I fancied an actual glow rising from the woman, though this was doubtless just another effect of Tuscan light. "*Boh!*" she huffed, turning the branches this and that way, fingering the pippins, of which there seemed an enormous number. "*Boh!*"

That expletive, many-valued in Italian, in this instance meant something like our *Aha!*

She beamed the whole while.

※

I feel joy when early autumn comes to upper New England, or rather a quasi-religious enthusiasm, containing several kinds of pathos. This has partly to do with the ritual reiterativeness of my preparations: I clean and reclean my shotgun, unlace and dress my boots, slathering grease into each crinkle and groove; I buy new collar-bells and fix them to new collars; I dust the army-surplus ammunition boxes and place them in the truck just so, between the dogs' crates and their water jugs. That sort of thing.

It will delight me once more to hear the *tonk tonk tonk* of the bells down in a bottom, watch sun-spangled leaves flutter earthward as I hike to bird covers known only to me and my best loved friends, see September's asters go brown with October, dropping to mulch as winter creeps close. I'll watch the season's first flakes sail past, hills darkening an instant when snowclouds gallop over. All this will have happened before, and will still be worth adoring.

And on the same days, for all their deep familiarity, something will present itself that in all my outdoor hours I've never before witnessed: a grouse taking refuge in a woodchuck den; my oldest pointer standing coondog-like, feet far up on a rotted oak (scent falling on so lowery a day) as a wood duck clatters out of her nesthole and across the beaver pond to westward; a roughleg hawk, rare in our parts (especially in this, his black phase), chasing down the bird I've winged, then hissing at my approach as if I were some runty pest, which perhaps I am.

Yes, as Angell says, there is beauty in an old game and a new season. May I be forgiven for punning on so marvelous a formulation, for my claim of rejuvenating beauty, too, in new game and an old season. Each grouse that flushes before my dog today is somehow the same one that flushed last autumn, and all the autumns before; but whenever those wings beat, each bird is also a fresh incarnation.

❧

Conclusions are my weak suit, always private and impressionistic, and in these ways maybe American too.

It occurred to me, as we began to pack for home, that my life is touched by some spiritual truth whenever I clasp hands with the generations of people who've done the things I do, and at the same time I keep a stalker's eye open for all the world's sudden turns. The day of my dreams is therefore one I'm often blessed to live, rising in an affectionate home, venturing into landscapes I treasure for their remoteness, returning. At my best, I'm a little barbaric *and* a little cultivated. Conservative and restive. Drawn to wildness for its own sake and to domesticating genius like that lovely Tuscan community's.

On our day of departure, I met Beppina in her olive grove. She did not unhand a certain branch even as we embraced. From a bit farther up the road came soft shouts—*li! qua!* An old peasant, bent and handsome, was coaxing matched oxen: they were white as New Hampshire snow against the limestone barn into which, just then, they were drawing the latest cutting of hay.

End of a Natural

WHEN IT WAS FINISHED, I sat in the truck for some while, staring at the clinic. Our veterinarians fashioned it from a modest old railroad station, but that morning the building seemed monumental, as if some mysterious force had both enlarged it and buffed away its eccentric, vaguely Victorian protrusions. "After great pain," wrote a great New Englander, "a formal feeling comes." I have discussed these lines of hers with innumerable college students and others, but I always forget their plain accuracy till circumstance reminds me.

Though Annie showed remarkable valor in her own pain, at length I needed to shut the suffering down. There hadn't been one cloudless patch on the final lung x-ray. She could no longer climb the stairs to my studio. She couldn't hold her bowels. Once so tireless in the field, she could barely hobble down our drive; then, rather than walk on, she'd turn from me and hobble back. Nobody might blame her. How had she so much as breathed, let alone brilliantly performed on grouse just a few months past? Now she was gone.

Another cycle: they get tighter with time; they set as if in stone.

After a last trusting glance, Annie took the injection, sighed, and went loose in my arms. I hadn't been able to contain myself then; yet sitting behind the wheel these few minutes later, I wouldn't have described myself as shaken. The formal feeling. I have it now and then after some brief illness. The fever breaks, and with a curious lucidity I think: I'm still here. In such instants, the world outside the windows seems splendidly composed, if disarming in its silence. Dawn will go down to day, day to starlight. Life will go down to death. But not yet for me.

The formal feeling also reminded me of other finales, particularly the close of some special hunt, or some special season, when I've been wondrously taken by a joy in the purely and factually given: These are my friends—Terry or Joey or Landy; this is my truck—six-cylinder stepside Chevy; this is my shotgun—Winchester Model 21, skeet-and-skeet; this is my hunting vest—tincloth Filson.

This was my pointing dog.

A south-to-north procession of crows, fighting the wind behind the vets' place, looked purposive. Things always take their course. By way of superstition, I once chose a puppy. She became my mature and canny partridge dog. She grew feeble and died. I could call that death untimely; yet what would *timely* be?

Across the Connecticut, I could see Black Mountain in New Hampshire. That delicate mauve of hardwood buds, just beginning to expect spring, had touched the mountain's flanks for centuries. Was wisdom sneaking up on me in the truck? If so, how did it differ from resignation, or were they the same? After years of Annie's blessed company, my philosophical mood all but shamed me; I suddenly wanted an agitation back, something as strong as that unboundable sadness of moments before.

For good or ill, I got my strange wish soon enough. Headed through the village, I came up behind a BMW with a sticker on its rear bumper. At first I couldn't quite read the words through February grime and highway salt; but when traffic slowed at town center I made them out: ANIMALS ARE LITTLE PEOPLE IN FUR COATS.

God in heaven.

Slayer of game, I know full well what judgments that driver would make on my character. I risk confirming them when I admit how tempted I was simply to drop into four-wheel drive and plow that fancy rig against the nearest pole. No ignorance piques me so much as my considerable own, but here was somebody else's for a change. I began to talk out loud: "Anyone who believes animals are people knows nothing about either." The usual drift. "Hell, *Hitler* hated blood sports. Where does that leave us?"

Did the driver ahead of me have pets? If so, I pitied them. A spouse or children? I pitied them further. But fury, not pity, ruined the composed, the formal feeling. By God, my Annie had never been little people! Just then I felt affected by this slogan as by someone's smirk at a passing funeral cortege. It was—yes—the lack of respect that enraged me.

Respect has forever been more important than affection in my attachment to my pointers and retrievers; or rather, it's been inseparable from the affection. Not that I don't love a pet. One dog always stays in our house, to be indulged with scraps, invited onto sofas, dragooned into kids' games. I suppose it's not so bad a life for that odd dog out (or in), but it doesn't earn respect like the working dogs' lives.

As I drove south toward home, passing old duck haunts and bird covers, ghostly in the mizzling late-winter rain, it occurred to me that my respectful feeling for the gun dogs is fundamentally the same as for the game we pursue together. One admires in a grouse or black duck the fact that it isn't degenerate, has lost no instinct. Likewise the furbearers. In the face of pressure from civilization, wild game has been genetically self-selected for qualities of alertness and evasion; just so, to keep pace the developers of working dogs have line-bred in order to distill, and not to transform or repress ancient traits. I've heard farmers call this or that cow "beautiful," but the idea's almost a scandal, as cursory comparison of the poorest whitetail to the finest Holstein proves. Shoo up the Holstein and watch her lumber off, swayspined, her great bags sloshing. She trails the olive drool of her cud. The chicken no longer even flies. But I'd chase deer or grouse for the mere privilege of beholding one get lost in a hurry, leaving me where I stand, slack-jaw. Even a fine-bred dressage horse isn't a patch on such beasts.

Similarly, look at a decent hunting dog move. Then watch the neighbor's pet. Both have been manipulated to be what they are. Yet although the hunter is sociable, even doting, there's a drive in that dog that will not be utterly and pathetically house-bound. To speak of training such an animal is almost a contradiction in terms: one's motive should be less to manage its instinct than to provide it the fullest opportunity to prevail.

If it can be said that my BMW driver "knows" animals at all outside the pages of books, can we doubt they are the house- or yard-bound ones? To that extent, let's grant a half-truth to his or her bumper sticker; for the degeneracy of such beasts is exactly the degree to which they've been roped into a world of little people. That beautiful cow is a milk-producing machine. That show horse struts its stuff in the least instinctive manner its rider can enforce. And what is the neighbor's pet if not fit emblem for consumerist culture? No one *needs* him (indeed he's a pain in the neck, even to his owner) any more than those cunning wares in the local mall's upscale boutiques. His function, simply, is to be bought and owned.

Of course I've hyperbolized, my recollection stirring exorbitant moods again. Needless to say, I'd often before encountered the silly sentimentalisms of so-called animal rights; but their inanity seemed especially assaultive just then, after Annie's death. Having known and loved that dog so well, I was angered, among other things, by the generality of the BMW driver's self-congratulation. The implicit claim of his or her bumper sticker was not to such a specific love for such a specific animal; it advertised love for all animals, as if there were no distinctions among or even within their species. What on earth could be the ground of such affection? If you "love" animals by virtue of imputing your own human traits to them, then you love not them but yourself. But which of your qualities can you attribute, say, to a silvertip grizzly? (And whom do you think you flatter?)

Walt Disney's *Bambi* having once brought this essential solipsism to large audiences, we're unlikely ever to be free of it again. Consider a moment from one of those unspeakable Benji films, in which the cuddly mutt chases a cuddly bunny to a stand and then—tears, I swear, glinting in his limpid eyes—"decides" he'd rather go on starving than kill so cute a creature. (Benji is scrupulous, I'd say, even for a little person.) Yet that turn must represent a beastly ideal for a certain camp. Henceforth, presumably, Benji will follow a vegetarian regime; rather than protecting his home ground, he'll attempt diplomacy; and be sure that by and by one of his selectively bred scions will actually start talking . . . of real estate, January white sales, miles per gallon, the United Way. I can't wait.

My trouble with all this may, I allow, be characterological. For instance, the very name of one troop—Friends of Animals—bewilders me, since in my experience friendship requires of us a *particularized* regard. What is true of friendship is even truer of love, which demands not only recognition but also affirmation of what the beloved in all honesty is. It demands, in a word, the respect I've mentioned.

A parable: I was once upbraided by a friend of the furry and feathery for shooting the local quail. I could only scratch my head. *There are no quail in our state.* Thus I must assume his commitment was not to any flesh and blood but to an abstraction. Some may take such a commitment seriously. I am not among them.

When I say I love the wild animals in a given ecosystem, I begin by acknowledging the plain fact that each must stand in relation to the others as predator or prey. The latter is not automatically less glorious than the former. (I am surely as thrilled by the springbok as by the African wild dog who brings him to earth, or, nearer home, by the wary Canada goose as by the gunner, however canny a scout and caller, who tumbles him.) Nor is any prey automatically pitiable, none being—to borrow a favorite rhetorical adjective from the Amoryites—"defenseless." That descriptive might indeed apply to what I'm calling degenerate animals, but I've yet to hear anyone use it who hunts truly wild game.

Even the miserable vole evades the great raptor more often than not.

Still, how do I rightly speak of love for the creatures I so frequently kill? Here I must again emphasize the part in that feeling of respect. Respect, precisely, for its nonhumanity; to deny that is simply to patronize. Animals are not people. (Little *or* big: our bumper sticker's very stress on the diminutive shows the patronizing touch; is a bull elk a little *anything,* for God's sake?) It's the otherness of wild animals, the hunters and hunted—and the residual spark of such otherness in certain companionable animals—that introduces unpredictable wonder into my psychic life as few things do in a world grown flatter by the hour.

The Alabaman's accent merges with that of the Minnesotan, which approaches that of the Vermonter, the New Mexican, the bureaucrat in D.C., the anchorman. The traffic light goes green and changes back. The job begins at 9 and ends at 5. April 15 is tax day, the second Tuesday in November election day . . . but why on earth was that grouse in the open woods, through which I'd been hiking to the *real* cover? The bird had its motives, but which? And once I reached that real cover, how did Annie know to quarter on the next bird so as to keep it from flushing through the protective hedge of fir, there at the border? I'd never trained her in such savvy, which was simply the crossing of her otherness with the prey's. What was yet wild in her intersected a wildness in her quarry, and, praise God, I was often there to witness. Even to participate.

True enough, before Annie was three, I saw she had it all. By then she'd taught herself to discriminate immediately between a running and a holding grouse and—depending on which was which—to lock up or rapidly trail, head high, eyes bright, till she had the bird pinned. The rest was up to me, and if I weren't confident that the best partridge gunners on earth have been in my shoes, I'd blush to admit my offense was too rarely up to the game's defense. Surely, we think, that bird will go *there;* but it goes elsewhere, too quickly for us to catch up.

Yet even the many Octobers when I shot like that, poorly; or when in a given autumn the game was scarce or the weather repellent—all those falls come back as good now, largely because there was always a dog in them, a dog to lead my life a small way closer to fusion with the life of their woods. As the trees have unleaved near season's end, the land gone stark, the sky taken on a hue that looks and almost smells like coin, I've had my pointers with me. Though I recall a distinguishing virtue (or, yes, vice) in each, sometimes they collectivize in mind: toward dusk, December waiting in the near wings, an Annie freezes on point at the top of a knoll. Backlit by a low sun, she assumes her predecessors, and even her successors. Her silhouette seems to grow larger and larger till it has the monumental quality of a classic sculpture. Or no—it's even cleaner than that—of such a statue's armature. Or no—since we're talking of wildness here—of the granite slabs I so often encounter in the back country, honed and grooved by climate, and by the passage over and through them of lively, untameable beings.

A Winter Grouse

A s FORECAST, the night brought a slight layer of snow. Today will be my final hunt for grouse this year: the game-cover is skinny, its feed depleted, and the scent's worse and worse in the cold.

Of course, I have the flu.

Recently, it seems, the first storm, the last day of a bird season, and this sickness have so perfectly coincided that I believe more than ever in the body's power of recall. My chest tightens, my eyes burn. They know how to mark an anniversary. I should lie in bed and recover, but there are other things to recover, to cover again—the covers.

"Colder than a frog's mouth," a neighbor says as we stamp by the general store's gas pumps. Across the common, Old Glory's blown straight as a plank. "Take two men to hold on one man's hat today," he adds. I've heard it before but I smile, happy to hear it again. Habit becomes me.

In short, though it'll be hard dogwork, hard hearing in such a gale, and though I'm ill, I'm content. The world is so crisp and honed I might be passing through some museum of The Beautiful, a commemorative place. Death of a season, but I'm perhaps like a person at the term of a bountiful life, who recognizes that the very prospect of death was what kept him keen to the bounty in the first place.

I know. All over the globe, desperate or despicable people unsheathe the billy or unfurl the electric lead, approaching the cell. Even after the Cold War's thaw, others contemplate throw-weight. Still others—the last of the bottle sucked down—turn on wife or child in a rage incomprehensible even to themselves. Not logical, exactly, the dream of available bliss I vaguely pursue as I set off along route 113; yet there it is, even if through my truck window I read the late history of nearby woods where I used to shoot. New "country estates" dot the hills. I must range farther each year, so much closing down around me.

Still my mood is affirmative, never mind the No Hunting posters on every tree. And never mind that this will likely be my last hunt in the Gore, which has been bought by the ski industry. Never mind that soon the winter sports enthusiasts will put up even more posters, hoping to save the wildlife they'll never see— *two thousand* condos planned in the Gore, each owner a friend of the game.

I bump my truck out of sight on the creamery lane. Just a cellar hole here now. I remember the proprietor's name, Hazen Flye. I remember the year he died, and how trim he left the place, and how soon it mouldered, the birds and animals flocking back to reclaim it. Instant ruin, full of romance. I vainly wish the same process on the whole of my territory.

Bessie shrinks and moans—the usual charade of suffering—as I fasten her collar-bell: then she races across the rough remains of Flye's meadow to loose her bowels. I step into the cover a few feet and wait. A woodcock, diehard, loiterer, whistles up. Along my barrels I watch him hover, and then sail over the road. When Bessie comes back, she locks on the little bird's scent. I call to her: "Gone."

This is a three-hour piece if I work it all. I have small faith that I'll move many partridge, smaller still that I'll get decent points, almost none that my bad ears will hear wings, but somehow I mean to travel over every inch.

Behind the creamery, land plummets into a patch of haw and twisty apple. I follow. A blaze flares from a trunk where a buck has hooked, and here and there the orange of rut shows in his pawings. I wobble on, downhill. Lord, I'm weak. It's going to be a *real* struggle coming out, but I'll worry about that when I have to.

The only sign of feed is a solitary thorn apple in a clump of untracked snow—perfectly red, perfectly shaped and displayed. I behold it a moment, then move on, pausing frequently in honor of my sickness and to pick up the sound of the bell. What a wind! More than once, I blow my lungs out on the whistle, so that the dog (close by after all) skulks, confused. What is bothering me?

Nothing, really. The sky is that dark blue I'd likelier associate with February than November. No cloud softens the prospect, but that seems part of the general rightness this morning: for instance, the abstract hardwood branches, rude as barbed wire, lovely.

Was that a grouse's flush? I don't know. I *think* so, but it may have been merely the hurtling air. I also think, when I come on Bessie, she has that slightly offended look she wears when a partridge has flown and no shot been fired. Was she pointing all this time?

I toot her on, losing the sound of her in an instant, noisy as I am on the frost, crunching past an abandoned hunter's shack, tripping once on a downed alder and crashing. I smile to recall the rage such accidents used to spark in me, how once I stood flailing my forearm at a hornbeam, as if that might avenge the indignity of a fall I'd taken.

No grouse among the grapevines below the shack. Why would there be, the grapes long since burst or bitten or buried?

I should take my usual route west through the remaining cover, but I feel an odd curiosity to find new ground, the chance of killing anything remote as it is. Younger, I'd have scoffed at the very idea of exploring on a closing day, especially in territory doomed by speculators. Maybe this morning I seek a farewell that's inclusive. I don't know.

I push on to a wide brook I've never before seen. Where on earth can it come from, go to? Bizarre country out this way. High, tawny grass riffles in the wind; I squint hotly at a near patch of it, ignoring the granite ridges to north and south: *This might be Africa, a lion crouched in that stuff, big tail flicking, dark stare on his face.*

An hallucination of wonder, not terror.

Since the water leaves me no choice, I do turn west now and follow the brook along its ice-beaded ledges. Bessie rushes past me. I can hear the bell for once, and can just make out her colors in the lion-cover. She stops dead forty yards on. What the *hell?* I consider the ground; it would be soft in a softer season, and I can believe that some woodcock might drop to it for a spell. But surely I saw the autumn's last woodcock up where I came in, wished him well, willed him to warmer climates.

So it's carelessly that I amble over to the point, and in complete surprise that I see the grouse flush. It crosses the brook in the hard light, bursts through a stand of tamarack, spilling dead yellow needles. I spill a few more with my tardy and hopeless shots.

I know that this winter I'll see that bird again in mind, almost black against the larch-gold. By sudden association I think, it's true what they say about fish: you remember The One That Got Away. My gun did not connect with this partridge, but somehow I had *him* on a line before he lost me. Just now I believe I pray for the snow to stay fluffy, for no fox to paw through an overnight crust, for the bird to keep busy till melt-time among high limbs decked in nourishing buds.

I swish through the wavy grass along the pristine stream, stopping once to watch a wild brook trout, who instantly darts under the cutbank. Perfect, that deep-green jacket, those vermilion dots, that shearwater shape. I feel a sudden and electric *expectation.* I know it has nothing to do with fish or even grouse, though I don't yet know I will see God within the hour—or more accurately, will see that I've been in His presence right along.

I turn north again, into the blow, against the swell of that hill I stumbled down at the start. The dog begins to make game, headed straight up, of course. It's a labor to follow, the flu like a flatiron upon my chest, each breath a bubble of phlegm, my legs no firmer than jam.

Enough. I must stop and sit, and I do, facing downward. A bird be damned: I'll find another; if not this year, then next.

My tracks in the snow-dust retreat into jackfirs. I follow them there with my eyes. I could rise and retrace them, seeing much on the way of what I've already seen this morning. But not all. To see it all, I must do what I'm doing, close my burning lids and recreate it. A teary impulse stirs at the back of my throat, not unpleasant. If I sat long enough, letting go, the mind's backtrack would take me through that strange yellow grass, across the frozen bottom by the dead hunter's camp, back up the hawthorn lane to the creamery's cellar cavity, where I flushed the woodcock.

It would also lead me through a thousand other thickets, up and down a thousand sidehills, around a thousand slues, over the thousand knobby apples that a thousand grouse once pecked at. I'd come on the points of many beloved dogs. I'd come on myself, maybe flailing my wrath against that hornbeam or casting down the empty shotgun after a miss on an easy straightaway. And I'd come on certain men, forever my age in vision but mostly gone now. Gone, or as one chooses to put it, used up.

Behind me, in the wind's momentary lull, a grouse rattles away. I'm sure of it this time. Bessie has been pointing, not twenty yards distant. Now she takes two steps, the bell barely clinking, and pauses. I whistle her ahead; she starts hunting again, never daunted. I get up and puff to the knoll's top, my gun shouldered, melancholy settled on me like a huge affirmation . . . which of course it is: after all, is it not a sign of life to mourn the passing of a joy and fullness we now and then discover?

I pause in the creamery meadow. The dung Bessie left as I waited under that hovering woodcock has already hardened. It marks where we started, and now, so soon after, she paces back and forth by the pick-up, wanting me to take her someplace where the action's livelier. She's only a dog, after all, a young one at that.

At the wheel I ponder which dirt road to follow. My doctor would recommend the easterly route, which leads straight home. The westerly circles to the Gore's far side, another big cover. But there's a third road that runs north for fifteen miles and *then* winds homeward. At twenty, flu be damned, I'd have ordered myself through that other big patch. In a different circumstance, I might still be angry at myself for not doing so now, precisely for not being twenty anymore. At sixty (if there are still places to hunt), I may on a similar day choose the home road. But for now I'm in middle way, as they say, which seems—in accord with the morning's mood—a good way.

This little middle-road tangle is almost square, and sits in the center of a timber yard, ancient and broad. Loggers once cut all the surrounding highland pine and oak, and there was nothing but ledge under the topsoil: the whole ridge turned to bone, its only growth a few maple whips. Why they left this square down below I don't know. Was there no market for the cedars that loom now over the sumac, ivory plum and barberry I'll stagger through?

At the northwest corner of the square the lumberjacks also left a hedge that juts uphill like the handle on a pot. A freshet runs through it in spring, but in fall you can hike up its bed, as I always do, because of a certain day in 1980. There were three of us. We knew, we know, each other's moves by heart: I handle the dog, Joey to my right and Terry to my left. I was running Gus then, a real ranger, and he had spilled out of the usual cover and come on point in the hedgerow. Joe crossed the brookbed, Terry stayed on the near edge, and I walked up the middle. The grouse had nowhere to go. There were six of them. We got them all.

Though we've never found another partridge in that row, we have religiously tramped its full length ever since, because whatever his conservation ethic—and ours is acute—a hunter wants just one time to realize a certain annihilative dream. So he may, though only that once and never again: still, the urge to retrace the path of dream and memory is irresistible.

Nothing but aching joints and hot gasps by now. I walk the dry brook to its upper end. Of course I flush nothing. Bessie obligingly works the strip, then breaks downhill toward the more likely cover. She is a rocket over the granite, with its spare adornments of maple sucker, lichen, ground pine. Head high, she cuts the rough, unseeable wind. I watch her grow smaller, and somehow whiter, as she approaches the thicket below. At the last moment I whistle; she wheels without breaking stride. I regard her, framed by the larger landscape—black softwood at cover's edge, two knolls behind it with their aspen fringes—and in this instant the air is invisible no longer. It shines, like the painted haloes of Quattrocento saints.

It is a blasphemy, even for a heretic like me, to have said I'd see

God this morning. And in any case it's not God I claim to see; it's His power and glory, which according to Paul are evident "in the things that have been made."

I pass in this fever of mine through what's left of the cover, slowly, and ever more so as I near the road. There will be no game in these last hundred or so feet. There never is. Yet I mean to protract the sense of a perfect end, for the long winter's coming, and what may be in or beyond it?

Again Bessie dances by the truck's door, anxious to try the birds in still another place, unaware that our hunt and season are done for. She whines her excitement, mouth gaped in a yawn whose climax is a vibrato squeal. The wind's still wide and urgent. Second growth tosses, clicks around me.

I look up, as we're taught to do in such moods, and there in a dead elm, for no reason at all, unless it's the one I surmise, perches the last grouse I'll see this year with a gun in my hand. I begin to raise the Winchester, speculating on which direction the bird will take when it flies. But it continues to sit, darkly outlined, motionless.

How long do I behold that grouse? I don't know. But at length the gun comes down. I break it, momentarily feeling the shapeliness of shotshells before I slip them into my vest.

If this were a true vision, I'd report that from that limb a voice thunders, demanding, *What manner of man art thou?* Indeed, though it makes no sound that an outer ear could hear, I do hear that voice. Perhaps to that extent this is—all of it—as true a vision as I believe, my gun cased, my dog crated, my truck following the snow-smeared lane back eastward.

Back to where I've come from today. Home and heat and family, and the young year's white coming months.

Presences

BECAUSE THE FISH must have weighed five pounds; because she'd been game beyond words; because she was a brown trout; because each little spot on her flanks wore its own pale halo; because of her shape's sleekness as I held her in the riffle till she recovered and swam back into deeper, unbroken water; because this was the fish I'd traveled for—I lay down in the Wyoming sun to nap. September-cool: not a cloud, not a biting bug.

The cottonwood deadfall on the gravel bar had composted, so that the trunk, once rough, now made a fine pillow. I put down my head, all full of the recent perfection. Because the moment had been the stuff of dreams, only dream could be adequate to it.

And I was tired: from the hike to the river; from the minutes in its water, which scarcely looked to be moving, but which was imperious when you stood in it; from the concentration that such a fish demands. I stretched out, convinced that some spiritual benchmark in my life had established itself, and that whatever might afterward befall me, I'd have it as an abiding reference.

What you see in today's dream, it's often said, relates directly to something in today's not-dream. Joey and I had roamed this country for a week, dawn till dark, without encountering so much as fresh sign of bear; but as I reclined, the sunlight just warm enough on my face, the sand smoother than any bed, the cottonwood pillow almost itself a part of slumber, the grizzly came.

We'd imagined him for days, and that was apparently enough, was a *way* of seeing him.

I don't mean that the animal was visible, nor that my sleep was really sleep so much as that half-wakefulness in which sensory detail seems both ordinary and eloquent of a different, a visionary realm.

I knew of the bear's presence because of the wind, which had doubtless been there all along—there as I approached the pool where the big fish and some smaller others were sipping those blue-wings; there as I laid down the cast and my fly drifted over the brown trout's lie and she shot up to have at it.

But in the midst of the stalk and the battle, my mind didn't register the sound, huge air forcing its way through high gaps. Though the air didn't move on the beach where I lay, the passes above were full of somber glissandi, like the musical theme in a frightening film that portends The Awe-Inspiring Thing. And what out here would that thing be besides *ursus horribilis*?

Even now I believed I could hear the scuff of his pads on the sandbeach, the faint cough of surprise at my scent. He needn't charge but simply and casually walk, all mammoth head and shoulders, to where I lay; then he'd paw me from under the deadfall like a grub.

No sense for me to bolt—this is an animal that can outsprint a bloodhorse—especially in my heavy, ridiculous waders. You're supposed to climb, because a grizzly doesn't choose to do the same. But the only tree within fifty yards was the fallen one under which I huddled now, almost awake. This was still mostly a dream, I could pray, and so maybe in slumber I looked dead. Because that's the last recourse when the grizzly addresses you: play dead. Joey and I had joked about this. Sure: play dead while eight hundred pounds of mammal thunders over the earth, the froth from his maw trailing in the breeze, glinting in the last of sun you'll ever see.

All nonsense, of course. I woke to a water ouzel, disappearing now and then under the surface to fossick for bugs; to an eagle's high screams, faint in the windy clamor; to the purr of the river where it swung through an elbow.

Yet there had been a presence. I am sure of it even now. Perhaps it was facile to associate it with Bear, but there'd been something.

I once thought to make a cartoon of myself. Its first panel would show me in woods or moving water, grasping a gun or rod; in the thought balloon over my head I'd be sitting before a typewriter. In the second panel, you'd see me before that same typewriter, but the thought balloon would show me standing with gun or rod in woods or moving water. For I am a man, by turns, in the outdoors with his head full of books and words, and a man in books and words with his head full of the outdoors. Yet I hope that at moments these men are merged, even if such moments exist in my poems alone.

One day—about eight weeks after the wind-driven vision of that Wyoming grizzly—I sat for hours, writing at something without much success. In my frustration I began to meditate on what now and then seems the paucity of milestones in my life. Such self-pity is a loathsome defect of my character: what better monument after all might I leave than my children, the second of whom, a daughter, ten years old at the time, had chosen this day for a house party? I'd stayed at home as token chaperone: Erika's guests were all female schoolmates, well behaved, completely capable of amusing themselves as young girls do—with chat, inventive games, humor.

After the first hour of the party, I saw my irrelevance to it, and perhaps my intrusion. So I advised the kids that I'd be in my office if they needed me, as of course they would not.

Perhaps I needed *them*. In the absence of their patter and shuffle—or the presence of my typewriter's mocking silence— I inwardly moaned that this was a day neither fish nor fowl. I might have gotten an angle on that piece of poetry and been by now some way toward its final draft; but no. I might have abandoned the project and taken myself outdoors; but not that either.

And now I recognized that this fall I'd spent less time than usual outdoors, fewer hours pursuing the grouse among draw, covert, sidehill. The wild provender in my freezer was not what it's normally been. The end of shotgun season loomed; I'd have to count on a deer. The bare shelves downstairs became, in this mood, an ungainly metaphor.

But surely all this just signaled slow blood. I simply needed some action, and if it could not come in verbal form, I'd go perspire. I find sweat an almost totally reliable curative. Having checked to see that he was at home, I wrote down the number of a neighbor and told my daughter and her friends I'd be back soon. They nodded distractedly, then turned again to the play they were rehearsing. I made to complain about how they'd dragged their props—cookware and clothing and bedcovers—into the living room, but thought better.

When I unlocked the kennel doors, the dogs nearly bowled me over. The younger and quicker of the pointers threw gravel at the end of our driveway, leaning into the corner down the woods road. I tooted her halfway back on the whistle, not wanting her out of earshot. The retriever, as usual, made a short dash, lifted a leg, then rushed back to be patted, and the older pointer, grown more meditative than her kennelmate with the hard-working years, pottered and nipped, in that inexplicable doggy way, at a few remaining stalks of grass.

I jogged, carefully, the dogs dashing back and forth by my legs. It had sleeted the night before, then lightly frozen. There were patches of ice along the twitch road, which runs downhill from home a few hundred yards. Where it peters out, there's something like a northward trail—made by game, by me and my dogs in our rambles—to the top of Stonehouse Mountain. It climbs 1800 feet in less than a mile, over slippery, lichen-covered granite. The soil here pushed settlers out almost as they arrived, their labor fragmentarily evident in stone fences that show all through the woods; occasional boulder-banked cellar holes; barn foundations; a rusted bolt or the spirit of a sugar vat or a hinge.

I made my way at a pace just properly taxing, so that the blood coursed in my ears and my breath came in rhythmic heaves. To make them shed their ice and straighten out of my way, I knocked at the bent saplings before me with a staff.

The therapy was working. I dropped my outer shirt by the side of the trail. I'd make a loop, then fetch it on the way home. My undershirt went wet with the forest moisture, but also with my own, which was what I'd been wanting. I thought how the poem left in my typewriter might write itself out here, if I made sure not to think about it.

I'd had certain things happen, or not, for years.

My legs felt strong and my wind full. I was a long way from dead.

☙

High air when I dreamed the bear, and more air to come. I gulped it that morning of my daughter's party. But just now I'm back in a different season from the same climb. Uphill, the woods are between the trillium—which have collapsed into their own cadaverous rankness—and the wild ladyslippers, little smug burghers that salute the birth of true summer.

But never mind such poetical cant for a moment, for I am also recently back from burying Larry, whose lungs had finally been borne down by the cancer in them, and in everything else, it seems, but his brain, which stayed clear to the end.

I first knew Larry when we both were three. He grew into a freckled, blocky Irishboy, tough and volatile. At length the toughness and volatility got mixed up with much too much booze, and he turned into a mean young man—then a middle-aged bum, flimflam, mess. Five years ago, he phoned me, drunk enough to call at 3 A.M., lucid enough to scream that he was in trouble: he'd awakened the morning before on an interstate highway, unsure whether this was Florida or Georgia or Alabama, whether the car was bought or stolen or borrowed.

What could he do?

I told him he could opt to die or not to.

For two years, I took other such phone calls, always in the middle of the night, the words slurring through long distance static. When I got the last of these rescue signals, I summoned up what little hardness I had: "Larry, I don't want to hear from you again unless you haven't had a drink for twenty-four hours." The phone clicked, and I lay awake, wondering if he was as suicidal as he claimed.

A year went by, and I heard from him again. I listened with my best ear as he got through the small talk. His voice had a crispness greater, even, than when he'd been a healthy, hell-raising kid, back in our school days.

"You haven't had a drink," I said.

"Not since the last time I talked to you." I could picture the old smile that made his freckles swim.

We stayed in touch, by mail and phone, through the short years after. The poor man couldn't get a break, yet he was sticking it out.

He was a grocery clerk when he was diagnosed.

Larry had felt sick since mid-winter, but he'd needed to work long enough to get company medical insurance before he could afford to see a doctor. By then it was too late, though it would probably have been in any case.

"*Where* is the cancer?" I breathed into the telephone, horrified.

"Where *isn't* it?" he answered. "Liver, lung, bone. . . ."

"It makes me lonely all over."

"It'll be all right."

"But it's sad."

"Sure. But there could have been something sadder."

"What?"

"I could have died the way I was."

I didn't see him again; he was gone before I could get to the city where he lay. And in fact, before he died I came to think of his cancer for some reason as a city itself, slum-infested, beyond any law. I pictured the breeze-blown detritus: plastic wrappers, cinders, tabloid pages. I envisioned the morass of grime from which winked broken wine bottles, shards of ruined windshield, those little sharp poptop keys. The disease was an inner urban sprawl, menacing figures in every aperture and alley.

Yet an angel came to that city. An angel and one other.

Before we buried Larry on that cloudless May afternoon a few days ago, all his friends from school years gathered at the plot, his brother announced to me a strange thing or two. He reminded me first, however, that although his pain was overwhelming, Larry turned down morphine, insisting that his head remain clear.

At 6:45 he told his brother that their mother—dead long since from cancer herself—stood in the room. She was not visible, he explained, but she was there, and she bore a message of assurance.

Just a few minutes later, the mother left and Jesus arrived. Or so Larry claimed; then he turned to that Presence, whatever it was, and said "I love you."

At seven in the evening exactly, Larry died.

At the same hour, Larry's sister was stabbed seven times by an assailant in her bookshop. She survived; indeed, she was standing among us at the burial ground. And after the funeral, another friend of ours told me how a light had followed him as he walked from his office to his car at seven o'clock. Yet another told how he'd had an appointment that day in Pittsburgh, how he'd mis-read directions, how he'd pulled over to roadside at the scheduled hour—seven—and concluded that he was lost, forever, beyond recall. Then I remembered the sudden exhaustion that came over me at the identical hour, when my wife and I always read to our three-year-old before putting him to bed. I slept a sleep like death till nine the next morning.

I make no elaborate case here. I seek neither to persuade anyone of anything, nor even to assert that my life has changed—for it likely hasn't: it seems, yes, that they arrive, those spiritual benchmarks in a life; one pledges to attend to them; and at length one goes right on as ever.

Though many of us survivors had drifted out of touch with one another, as with Larry, over the decades, we quickly fell into the old closeness—no, it was a greater closeness, the posturing of male adolescence corrected not only by our aging but also by the dead man's final heroism and serenity. *His* was the Presence of that day, its genius.

❧

I do not climb for the view alone, since I've got it by heart. Indeed I almost prefer to climb into fog, the kind that cloaked the mountaintop in the forenoon of my daughter's houseparty. I felt as though I'd stepped into another element altogether, as though I were underwater but able to breathe. Such a thought lifted me back to the Wyoming streamside, to the moment when the brown trout—having taken my little dun, having fought with the cour-age of wild things against me—quivered for a minute or two in my hand. A moment before I let her go back to her pool. Before the bear arrived.

I can *will* such details into memory if I choose; but I prefer them to recur by means of some unexpected, unwilled association as they did on Stonehouse Mountain, the day's wetness suddenly transporting me. The spots on the fish's belly and loins reappeared in mind, each brighter than new-minted coin, each distinct, and—a thousand and more miles away—the air I breathed became freighted with the scent of western rapids and hot stones and fly repellent and bison dung, as well as with the glorious odors of the White Mountains where I lived. And they and the Wyoming mountains I'd visited rolled together and life seemed all it could ever be.

Coming out of my reverie, I noticed a dainty doe's track through the frost that lingered above two thousand feet. She had crossed the trail on tiptoes; just then I preferred that print to a heel-heavy buck's for a sign. Coarse and heavy myself—bearded, two hundred pounds, sweaty, my boots all mire—I was in the domain of delicacy.

I did not worry for my dogs; they'd long since been deer-broken. They champed and thrashed in the understorey to either side as I stooped and read the doe's track, fresh enough to fill with fogwater as I beheld it. I closed my eyes, and the fish swam through that water, and the stream out west flowed into it, and it reflected that overhead glory of an early Teton fall, so deep it's something other than blue.

But I was an ignorant man, and I still am.

Uphill forty more yards, two granite slabs leaned together, making a cave. There was no evidence yet of traffic in and out. Come winter, it would shelter a fox or perhaps a second year cub. Just now, I fancied it underwater too, and my fish peering from it, suspicious.

At home, the schoolgirls were play-acting. I imagined them as mermaids, or water sprites. Why not? Uninvited to their free-form drama, I could go on surmising that their visions, like mine, were aquatic today, even though at this time of year I'd normally be preoccupied—in imagination and action alike—with earth and air. It was still legally hunting season for birds, crouching on the woodsfloor, leaping into low sky before my pointers. But water it was, even though there'd be a long, hard winter before the run-off, the spate, the ebb, the occasion to look for a trout nearby.

Perhaps my thoughts ran as they did because I couldn't have hunted in any case. Not only did I have to be roughly within summoning distance, nine girls in my house and my wife and our other children away for the day, but also the going would have been too hard for me and my dogs. It's one thing to take an hour or so and follow a trail, however sketchy, to the top of a mountain; it's quite another to break through sodden, icy brush all day.

I'll let the shotgun season die in peace, I concluded, and—that resolve turning me melancholy again—I forged on. The sweat had started to cool, and I was breathing too shallowly. My fish had swum into her cave again, and when I willed her out, she looked different, like an exhibit in some tawdry sporting museum. I let her swim back in.

My younger pointer bitch shot across the trail ahead of me, leaping her slower brace-mate, who trotted the other way. Each cast an eye toward me, checking in. "All right!" I called, and they hurried on. Yet I thought suddenly how I'd missed the retriever for a few minutes. He wouldn't have gone far; he never does. But having once lost a dog on such a hike—he got out of hearing, he never came back—I'm more cautious even than I need to be.

I gave four short, quick blasts on the whistle, and waited. Two more minutes went by, and I was mildly unnerved. He is the most reliable, the most companionable, the least rangy of my three. I blasted again, and again I waited. Two *more* minutes, and no retriever.

This went on. I had last seen him fifty or sixty yards back down the trail. I dropped my plan to get to height-of-land; that peak would abide forever, but a dog is mortal, and now suddenly I wanted him more than anything on earth.

My soul ached for a dog . . . who showed himself in the next instant, by the side of the trail, near where I'd left him a few minutes ago. I scowled and bellowed his name and shrilled at the whistle. He lifted his muzzle momentarily, then, hunching his shoulders and grinning in that manner of a dog embarrassed, he disobeyed me, lowering his head again to whatever it was he sniffed there by the mossy, overturned basswood.

I lifted my stick as if to threaten a beating, but he kept busy with something—something no doubt extraordinary, because he is the most biddable of dogs and never resists me. I stood stock-still for a moment, perplexed: this is a duck dog, a retriever, but he might for all the world have been pointing just then, at whatever it was, flattened to blend with the umbers and beiges of the late-fall carpet.

Suddenly I heard that mid-range howl of wind I recalled from the day the dream-bear approached. It must have been blowing between the tops of Stonehouse and Mousley right along, but my crunching bootsoles and my heavy breathing and my water-fantasies must have deafened me to it, even if the trees and the brush were all sideways now in the gale. Since there is scarcely a thing in the New England woods besides the woods themselves to hurt you, I can't say what I felt, hearing that music again: maybe only the vestige of a fear felt in another place.

I walked the few steps to my dog. He had something, all right, though he had not taken it up in his mouth. I squatted and saw that it was the severed tail of a red fox, which, despite the dull gray of a cloudy autumn, glinted brightly, its ice-beads like pearls.

The sleetstorm of the preceding night had buried whatever sign might have surrounded this foxtail, and there was no trace of the rest of the corpse. Does the animal trot somewhere even now, ridiculous without his fine brush? Or is he dead and devoured almost entire, nothing left but this muff of hair over frail bone, splendid, bejeweled? And what might have killed him? A fisher, a lucky bear or coyote, a rover dog?

The sound of the wind in the pass was louder and louder, or was it my thoughts that made the crescendo?

It was beautiful, that unbloodied remnant, full with the imminence of white winter, a deep scarlet with undertones of silver. I thought of my daughter Erika, and how I must bring this bolt of fur back to her and her Thespian troupe. I imagined their widened eyes. Perhaps Erika would want to hang it in her room. If not, I thought, I would nail it to the shed wall between the two kennel doors. It would look good there.

But as I reached to take the foxtail up, the wind's roar moved to a still louder pitch, and I could not lift what I meant to lift. I contemplated it, rather—long and sleek, like the body of that trout I'd released. The wind still bore an uncertain burden. I straightened, my eye yet fixed on the dazzling fur before me; but in my lateral vision, there was something I could almost see. I could certainly feel it.

I remain an ignorant man, far too much so to say I was touched then by any spirit from the natural world, the human world, or any imaginable other.

But something was there.

IV

Alone, with Friends

Alone, with Friends: From a Journal Toward Springtime

THERE WAS ONCE a woodsman, the kind you'll meet less and less often from now on. I think of him constantly, and never without breathing the woodsy odors of his native low-country Maine. Funky leaf-mulch, black swamp, tannin in the waters. Or I listen to the chatter of a moosebird (as he called the gray jay), hopping sideways onto our lunch ground, the wingboom of nighthawks that slash through a crowd of hatching mayflies. Or see the autumn line gales whip downlake, the smoke from his camp on the first hard-frosty morning, a wedge of duck over Smith Gulch. Whatever. And mixed with all that, his voice, oddly high-pitched yet husky. Always his voice, blessed column of air that bore these and other particulars, pushed them up into story.

The woodsman was Creston MacArthur, and I loved him like a blood relative. After his funeral, wounded, disoriented, I went out to visit Earl Bonness. Though considerably older than Creston, he'd been his closest friend, and with him had driven logs, trapped, hunted and swapped counsel for four decades. I expected no immediate consolation, but I knew somehow I'd hear a proper valedictory.

Earl found it even more cruelly hard than I to speak. Our quiet went on and on, till at last his thrilling bass, more mournful than ever, broke into it: "I judged he was sick; but I didn't judge he'd die."

Carpenter, Mechanic, and I:
it is our yearly hunting trip
to this game-rich, splendid, dirt-poor margin
of Maine. There is always rain and a gale,
and one or two
bluebird days just to break the heart.
We're good at this thing we do,
but for each bird that falls,
three get by us and go
wherever the things that get by us go.

To the realm of baby shoe and milk tooth;
kingdom of traduced early vow,
of the hedge's ghost, humming with rabbit and rodent,
under the mall's macadam. All that seemed
fixed in the eye. I,
according to Mechanic,
is too melancholic. Yes, says Carpenter,
and talks when he ought to be doing.
We all watch the canny pointer, with her nose
like a Geiger counter.

"There's not much gets by *her*,"
we repeat each year, admiring, after she's flashed on point
and *shaaa!*—in redundant wind another grouse flies wild.
Air and ridge and water now all take
the color of week-old blood. Or years-old ink.
We are such friends it's sad.
Not long before we stalk before winter the heavy-horned
bucks that slide past,
spirit-quiet, in spare brush.
Then Carpenter and Mechanic in their loud mackinaws will seem

interruptions on the skyline of the sky's
clean slate. And so will I.

I myself judged that these weren't final words, and so held my silence. Finally the old fellow rose from his workshop chair. Half mending the stoop of his back on the way, he walked to the door, kneed it open, and looked out across the deep February snow. Past standing-dead cornstalks in the garden. Past the hound's run. Past the barn to the hair-dense woods, which seemed, as ever, poised to swallow the paltry homeplaces along the Tough End lane. Just east, the river hummed under its ice. At last Earl turned, very close to weeping but not: "We made a lot of tracks together."

3/4/1992

I recorded the preceding entry last month, and sixteen years to the day from Creston MacArthur's death. Likely no more than coincidence, for it was only after some reflection and calculation that I recognized the timeliness at all. On the other hand, why shouldn't my gesture suggest an *instinctive* anniversary impulse? In what follows I'll imagine that it did; and that instinct pointed toward matters (not connected exclusively nor perhaps even primarily with Creston) that have long lain in partial hiding; and that I can root them out—write them out.

"We made a lot of tracks together."

If Earl's words did not quite move him to tears those years ago, they did me; and did again a few weeks back; and do as I recall them here, no matter that *here* for the moment is almost as far from that little shed, at least spatially, as I could go in the western world. I'll return to Earl, to Creston, to others like them. I must, for reasons literary and otherwise. But I'll be patching these notes together in Budapest.

3/11

I am not low on cash, thanks to the Hungarian ministry of culture and the United States Information Service, who conspired to arrange my visiting professorship of American Literature at the city's largest university (and in the process reminded me, as if it were needed, that I'm no Bonness nor MacArthur myself). I'm not lonely either: what more comforting company than a beloved wife and children? And only be inexcusable exaggeration could I call this apartment a garret. Yes, it sits on the uppermost floor of our building, but the real estate agent—one of the neighborhood's sudden, eager entrepreneurs—rightly counts that to be among the flat's several attractions. We have a view of the chalk-streaked Buda hills on this side of the Danube, and of humming Pest on the other. Ours is an atypically quiet block, close to the efficient public transport but removed from the worst of the city's unspeakable pollution.

No poverty. No solitude. No chill, roachy closet at the top of gruesome stairs. (Nothing that in my youth—and needless to say in Paris—I believed essential to a writing career.) Why then this feeling of bereavement after mere weeks? It has partly of course to do with missing a few people, along with my dogs, my waters, my woods. The only wild creatures hereabouts all pent in the national zoo, there are moments when the common naggings of a common red squirrel in a common hemlock would positively exalt me: I mourn at being pent myself, town-bound just as the spring freshets must be *un*-binding themselves, yelping down the mountains, chasing the home countryside into music.

I try to buck up by imagining virtue in such minor forlornness. Maybe it will turn out that my soul's history, odd congeries of books and beasts, schools and sidehills, writing and rivers, solitude, friendship and a family that's by now a crowd—maybe that inward history will reveal itself more steadily and whole while I'm so removed from the region where it has unfolded. In that case, these notes will be worth the making, and this dull daily ache the enduring. In the early phases of my hunt for so round a vision, however, I find myself touching a pain of exile that shouldn't keep surprising me as it does.

No native backcountry Yankee, early in life I learned at least to *talk* Bonness–MacArthur. I'm a quick study with foreign languages, and so have been a pretty carefree tourist in the past, sometimes nearly persuading myself I wasn't a tourist at all.

Magyar, however, proves intractable.

I'll admit to fair warning: getting word of this Fulbright appointment, I immediately telephoned my friend Walter Arndt, estimable author and translator, to ask who might teach me the host nation's tongue. After a pause on the line, there came a sound that somehow married snicker to sigh: "Sydney, there is no one on earth who can do such a thing."

"But surely *you* speak Hungarian," I protested, mindful that Walter commanded not only his native German and its relatives but also each Romance and Slavic language, with Turkish and God-knew-what-else thrown in.

"I once tried." Pure sigh this time. "But it was too hard."

I shivered—appropriately, as it now seems.

3/13

Hungarian is an inflected language, rife with unfamiliar cases, peculiar word-endings. Manageable stuff, to be sure, if it weren't for other obstacles: the fact, say, that prepositions simply don't exist, their values assumed by a host of mind-boggling suffixes, all of which must work—so to speak—to, from, with, near, on, around those cases. There are likewise countless verbs with both transitive and intransitive forms, and factors dictating use of this one or that seem terribly obscure now and then. Finally, the slightest slip-up in pronunciation proves even more disastrous than in other places (with what embarrassing ease, for instance, can one's wife become one's half-ass, a bus the love act, on and on). Yet none of these problems, nor the remaining hundred and some, would spell curtains for a western child if only this were, as it's not, an Indo-European idiom. Magyar's one sure kinship is to Finnish, scholars arguing about other relations—to Moldavian, say, or Korean, or certain dead dialects from the now dead Soviet Union.

Lord knows I can't have an opinion on any of this. I can't so much as validate my frequent impression that the Latin or Teutonic cognates in Hungarian might be counted on two hands, fingers left over. All I know is that such languages as I have are more impediment than aid to me, no matter how simple and singular the word I search: if I ask for *milk, milch, lait, latte, lece,* I progressively mystify the local seller of *tej.* My children's thirst for ice cream must be quenched by *fagylalt.* And we haven't yet gotten past dairy products.

For the first time in life I am reduced to hand signs and grunts; and, still more agonizing, at least once a day I excuse myself from prospective conversation: *Nem ertem,* I mutter. I don't understand.

3/18

Consignment to muteness by turns grieves and angers a man who's talky to a fault in company. Still hoping that necessity can mother virtue, however, I've been dreaming of Budapest as a laboratory, of this journal as a set of experimental notes on the efficacy and the limits of language. By vocation, I've supposedly pondered such issues throughout my adult life . . . yet never, I concede, with quite the same desperation: the strangeness of words all around me serves to concentrate the mind wonderfully, as Dr. Johnson once said of a death sentence. And in fact I discover that this dumbness does feel almost like punishment.

Sentenced to sentencelessness, *peine forte et dure.*

I begin partly to see why my first entry, which impels all the rest, recalled an old friend—adored, lost.

3/20

Two days pass, full of more tongue-tied frustrations, and all the while I almost hear the ironic chuckles of certain trendy academicians. There's one such fellow, another visiting American, at my university—a hell of a nice guy as it happens, and too bad: he half dismantles the perfectly good pile of animus I've been building. (My lust for conclusion seems always to come up against these annoying obstacles.) In any case, since many of today's hip critics argue that words are after all only units in arbitrary systems of sound—"free-floating signifiers," to echo the buzz phrase—they might consider this Hungarian ordeal, however galling to unhip folks like me, a mere reminder of dowdy truths: that speech is never truly communicative, that "meaning" is a sentimentality. I guess this means (if I may) that the syllables I heard on the subway an hour ago were ultimately no more unintelligible than those of George Bush (it's primary season back in the States)—a conclusion I almost accept; but the example is poor.

My perspective is conspicuously an outsider's, never more so than now. Yet it still seems odd that, in proving the arbitrariness and meaninglessness of words, the insiders spend such a lot of . . . words, presumably arbitrary and meaningless too. Moreover, for all their self-labeled progressivism, the modish academicians can also commit downright mischief: how many of my Hungarian neighbors would agree, for example, with one Big Daddy of contemporary theory, Jacques Derrida, who once called freedom too attenuated a term to have any meaning for *them*? And it's likewise strange that in their mission to "de-privilege" traditional notions of authorship, the new dons belabor truths that any author in any tradition grasps within a few moments of starting seriously to write: literary characters are not real people; different readers bring different responses to what they read or hear; and above all, words—however refined and congregated— are exasperatingly tricky, often "succeeding" in unintended ways and similarly failing.

And you needn't even be a writer to see the word "raspberry" (*malna* over here) and know you can't *eat* the goddamned thing.

❦

It was a slow morning for me and Creston in our Mutton Cove duck blind, fall of 1969, hard wind coming west through the gap in the Middleground, pushing waves right to our feet, almost swamping the decoys. We turned therefore to conversation, just this and that, till at last I decided to explain the subject of my Ph.D. dissertation, a jargon-ridden inspection of certain narrative dilemmas. When my talk petered out, Creston said, "Sounds like hoss-shit with a coat and tie."

Yet he did love a story. And his narrative technique was flawless.

3/25

There are obvious reasons why I should be called a visiting professor at Eötvös Loránd University. And yet, whatever and wherever my college or university connections, professorship seems more and *more* a visitor's estate for me. Once an aspirant scholar, I lately cultivate what even the highbrow T. S. Eliot calls the poet's "necessary laziness," willfully falling out of touch with academic-intellectual wrangles, on which my judgments, if any, must be more or less intuitive. Thus have I half blundered onto certain controversies in this journal; and thus I infer, for example, that the chief distinction between the Contemporary Author (assuming such a singular beast) and (likewise) the Contemporary Literary Theorist is a temperamental one. The principals agree that no poem or essay or novel, let alone conversation, will ever entirely finish the job of plain, uninsidious communication. From such simplism, Theorist—oddly, a bit like the Puritan fathers I've lately been discussing in a Hungarian tutorial—concludes that literature is deceptive, even harmful. And so, Let it come down. Let it be, as they say, deconstructed. Author, on the other hand, is goaded by the inevitable imperfection of his or her work: Let's try again, and again, again, again, again. Let's build the damn thing right this time, *con*-struct it.

I'm not keen on Puritans, but for now I won't insist on the superiority of the writerly temperament to the theoretical. In fact, since I happened to talk about it today in another class, I'll mention a work by our clumsiest national genius Theodore Dreiser, less well known than it deserves, which speaks exactly, nor altogether approvingly, of an author's awakening.

"Nigger Jeff"—as the tale is unhappily called—concerns a certain Davies, a reporter, smug with inexperience. Davies is sent to cover the aftermath of a racial crisis. The title figure has

drunkenly molested a farm girl and, before trying to escape, come
home to see his family; he is captured there by the town sheriff,
and shortly afterward lost to a lynching party. The reporter goes
to see the victim's corpse, and is moved as never before by the
mother's speechless grief, in face of which "his intrusion seemed
cold and unwarranted":

> Out in the moonlight he struck a brisk pace, but soon stopped and
> looked back. The whole dreary cabin, with its one golden eye, the
> door, seemed such a pitiful thing. The weeping mammy, alone in
> her corner—and [Jeff] had come back to say "Good-by!" Davies
> swelled with feeling. The night, the tragedy, the grief, he saw it all.
> But also with the cruel instinct of the budding artist that he already
> was, he was beginning to meditate on the character of the story it
> would make—the color, the pathos. The knowledge now that it
> was not always exact justice that was meted out to all and that
> it was not so much the business of the writer to indict as to
> interpret was borne in on him with distinctness by the cruel sorrow
> of the mother, whose blame, if any, was infinitesimal.

We can each think what we like about Dreiser's program for art
here. One clear thing, though, is that the voyeurism he alludes to
comes with art's territory. And there was never a halfway accom-
plished author so conscienceless (I hope) as not to feel some of
Davies's remorse at it.

Drafting a poem on the early death of my younger brother, I
remember an abysmal self-loathing, as if I'd somehow said out
loud, "Good—now I can write something powerful." Yet I could
not turn away.

No writer can turn away. Each, however secretly, approves
Davies's cry from the heart:

> "I'll get it all in!" he exclaimed feelingly, if triumphantly at last.
> "I'll get it all in!"

That mission to omni-inclusiveness, as any author knows, is
impossible this side of the grave (which is why an Edgar Allen Poe
bothered to hoke up something like "Ms. Found in a Bottle,"
supposedly scribbled in the very passage from life to death); and

yet—more than what's called talent—that mission *makes* a writer a writer. It also distinguishes our Writer, at least theoretically, from our Theorist, whose argument should lead him or her at length to silence, words being no better than silence after all.

Yet here am I: not including, but excluded; reduced to utter quiet myself.

3/27

If to be a writer meant I must give up the outdoor life and enter the world of books only, how would I choose? If to remain an outdoorsman meant I must abandon books, mine not excepted, what would I do? I can imagine more agonizing decisions in my personal life—but not a great many at that. Yet often it seems so hard to make sense of the two worlds together, even on revisable pages like these. I think of my writing as addressed above all to friends, but which? Earl Bonness? Walter Arndt? Each by turns? Must I ask one to stand by as I jaw at the other?

It is no trick to feel rather alone in this racket.

4/1

On the way to work this morning, I unintentionally jostled an attractive woman in the thronged tram. To judge from her look, it was probably an oath or insult she spoke to me. My response— the only available—was to remain silent. Later in the day, I carried our two-month-old daughter onto another packed car: native passengers, as smarmy over children as Italians, actually fought with each other to give up seats to us. They sought to draw me into those negotiations, but did they do so by remonstrating, cajoling, flattering, preaching? *Nem ertem.* I had to make my guess on the basis of what's called body language, none other at hand. At all events, I remained silent. And of course I felt an almost unbearable, physical impulse to speak out, the more so when, having done the arithmetic, the other passengers fell back into quiet themselves.

Although astonishingly friendly, those Budapesti could not be my friends. Not until we learned one another's verbal ways, which would probably take more time than any of us had left.

This evening I find myself searching for the difference between such jitneying and many a journey with partner Joey Olsen to our hunting shack in Maine. A builder, Joey is perhaps naturally more a man of deeds than words, at the very least compared to me. Yet there is something else in him, something deeply and atavistically New English, which emerges with a vengeance on the night highway. Hours and miles go by in which we exchange not a sound. During these lulls, oddly, my own talkative self takes its holiday too. This is, I'm sure, in part because each of us in the truck knows what the other is thinking about—the big, game-rich covers, unposted and unspoiled; the thrilling lock of a pointer upon her grouse; the drum-roll of the bird's flush; the scent of cordite on good fall air; hiss of a woodstove and smell of rude cooking. In any case, I seem to relish the ruminative quiet as much as he does.

However rare it is for me to practice such under- or nonstatement, I've long been curiously, profoundly attracted to it in the northcountry native son. (I'm drawn conversely to the garrulity of native daughters too, but that is stuff for different reflections, which would have to trace the probable history of this generic distinction, with at least a glance at some nearly forgotten but notable "local color" authors from the last century. All female— I've been reading them too over here.)

Why should a jabberer like me value the reticence unto pure quiet of a male Yankee? Why should it arouse so little of the frustration I feel in a nation whose people retreat into silence with me perforce? The simplest answers, of course, are that the Yankee *could* talk to me if he chose, however often he doesn't (to anybody), and that it's from these New Englanders—famed for *not* being particularly friendly— that I've chosen my nearest friends. And yet for all their very simpleness, these facts lead me further and further into musings on the very nature of friendship, above all its relations to speech. Or to absence of speech.

❧

Creston MacArthur's father and uncle were well-known poachers in the Depression years. They are both, like him, long gone now, but I can summon their voices when I like, and with them the odors of mackinaws drenched by lakewater, mist rising from their wool by the Round Oak stove in the Wabassus cabin. Wavelets tickle the beach in cadence. The uncle, George, has a manner of chunking the firebox, a quick little underhand toss that's always on the mark. Franklin, his brother, strokes the left side of his face in a certain way as he tells a story. He's stroking it now, recalling the two wardens who tried to catch him and George, out on Slaughter Point.

"They's building a camp near the flowage, special, just to watch us," Frank says. "Never knew *we* was watchin' *them* . . . but we was. Set right there in the Stone Dam woods to do it." He pauses, lengthily, spitting a bead of juice into the same old coffee can, which he settles back on his lap just so. "They drive the very last Christly nail with a broke pole-axe, then head for town on the clean jump, down to Paul's for their baloney and rolled oats and that-like."

Another long pause. George flips a split of soft maple, adjusts the draft, whistles softly, arms akimbo, smiles at the speaker.

"When they come back, that camp wa'n't no good to 'em."

Eighty words, give or take. Beginning, middle, and end. Though I've heard it before, I laugh loud and long. Then the quiet settles in again, but for the dear waters outside.

4/3

My daily schedule at home is scarcely that. Apart from the obligation to show up now and then on some campus, and apart from familial duties (copious enough, to be sure, if you're father to five), my hours are arranged pretty much as I see fit. In the autumn—to which, in a vast foreign city, my mind keeps turning—I see fit to spend as much of them as possible in the woods, shotgun at the ready. Since my very few hunting pals all work honest jobs, I tend except on weekends to have only my pointing dogs for company.

I do talk to those pointers; but they are even less chatty, even more all-business than northcountry humans. To use my region's highest accolade, they're Good Workers. Thus, if there's a ruckus of sound in my solo ventures—breeze, crunch of bootsoles, collar-bell, groan from a tree-trunk, rattling wings, periodic report of my Model 21—spoken commentary is scarcer than on those pilgrimages with Joey to camp.

My *inward* articulations, however, are ceaseless as rivers. I recite stories I've heard; I speak of how lightning has recently scarred a great pine that my friends and I have often used for a marker; I try to render into image the way of the dog on a certain cock partridge; I rave over the colors of a wild squaretail trout, guarding a spawning place in a spangly stream.

These mute remarks often turn out to be the very rough drafts, or partial drafts, of many a thing I'll come to write: this entry, for instance, in which, still searching for an overview, I realize that those silent monologues are also often the rough drafts of what I'll later share with a Joe, a Terry Lawson, a Landy Bartlett or David Tobey, next time I see any or all.

I am alone, with friends.

There is a continuity between my interior talk, what might generously be called my higher talk, and my friendly talk. I hope.

If for all kinds of reasons—personal, social, professional—I will never in friendly testimony invent something at once so eloquent and economical as "We made a lot of tracks together," and am not even sure I honestly covet such terseness, still I love the language there, and the *suspicion* of language. Although I may pull at least equally hard in some other direction, it's fine to feel the tug of that diction and attitude whenever I seek to record my thoughts and feelings, aloud or on the page. A comment like Earl Bonness's reminds me that metaphor need not be overwrought, that syntax need not appear "arbitrary" or convoluted, and above all that every property of language benefits from rootedness in a palpable, shareable context.

When, after his closest chum was in the ground, Earl looked from his shop to the woods, I knew he stepped into them in spirit, and Creston with him. The wind came from an auspicious quarter or not; on Dougherty ridge, just west, the broadleaf buds were starting to tinge the overstorey with purple; everywhere, waters were preparing to release themselves; out in the town cemetery, a moosebird tilted atop some knife-thin grave marker, seeking for purchase despite ice on the stone.

4/8

Scanning my last entry, I'm impelled to point out that the Yankee idiom is supple; it is not always, like Earl's, elegiac (except perhaps to itself, in an age of specialistic cant on one hand, mass babble on another). I recall a time in the early seventies, for instance, when a well-funded hippie briefly moved to our little town, cobbling together the requisite Cabin-in-the-Woods. The thing was an inevitable mess, and this young fellow (call him Phil) reconciled himself to hiring a local man (call him Dub) who actually knew how to build.

Phil, as they said in those days, was "heavily into meditation." He liked to practice his version of it at daylight—or at least at his version of daylight, which came several hours later than Dub's. In timeworn manner, the carpenter made sure to arrive on the job site while his client still slept; then he'd sit in a running truck till he'd gotten Phil out of bed. Every day at this point, Phil groggily invited the workman in, assuring him that nothing would disturb the subsequent hours of trance.

I met Phil myself during this repair stage to his hovel. I suffered his talk about how and why he meditated; the aim was to reach a condition of simple *being*, in which consciousness—and particularly all its attendant, equivocal, inward and outward verbiage—could be stripped away. Oddly enough, this explanation itself seemed extremely wordy; it seemed, moreover, merely a version of the Yankee's less elaborate assessment.

"So what do you think of Phil?" I asked Dub later.

"Ain't a lot *to* think," he replied. "He don't *do* nothin'. Just sets right there."

❦

It may be a long way from the foregoing anecdote to my ongoing reflections on the era's literary palaver—but maybe not. Just as our Theorist crowds page after inscrutable page with "proof" of words' ultimate inadequacy, which, as I've insisted, is instantly evident to any writer, so did Phil enter a verbal labyrinth to express an ultimately banal idea: that, to echo another Gallic hero

of contemporary theory, language is a prison-house in some
degree.

Language, however, is what we've got.

4/10

Today I suddenly worry that many of the preceding remarks
smack too much of good old American nose-thumbing at school,
for I have neither personal credentials nor desire to be entirely
skeptical of intellectualism, nor of dense, prolix language: I mean,
look where I am, what I do . . . and hear how I sound.

It is scarcely my claim that each last thing ever thought or said
by a professional thinker is something that's been more economi-
cally thought or said by an Earl or a Joey or a Dub. What Henry
Adams—who made for a pretty fair class this afternoon—did in
the *Education* is something none of these men could have done.
(Of course, I couldn't either.) It's only that so much of what I
lately hear from the academy, like those opinions on the limita-
tions and fatalities of literary "text," seems if not banal at least
obvious enough that these bumpkins do say it. More straightfor-
wardly, more colorfully.

I must anecdotalize as I must breathe. I was standing by George
Lawson's garage twenty years ago this past November, when a
woman drove onto the lot. Once the wife of a popular local man,
she'd left him for a poet whom she met at a Dartmouth College
reading. The poet sat on the passenger side—a fact which in those
days seemed to the likes of George a little disruptive of the world's
order to begin with—and, as the assistant mechanic Herbie filled
the gas tank, our poet played loud Motown music on the radio,
flinging his head, popping his fingers. After an awkward interval
for all concerned but the Motown fan, the woman drove off.

George came out to join us by the pumps. He and Herbie
looked colorful: it was deer season, and even during the working
hours each man wore blaze orange, which aptly clashed with the
fuel company's red horse logo on the garage wall. I remember
seeing a smart cedar waxwing in the blighted elm that loomed
over wrecks in the back field.

"So that's the one she run off on the husband for?" George asked, as if somehow it were all *my* fault.

I nodded.

"Dumb-looking bastard," Herbie opined. And then the operative question on both men's minds: "He *do* anything?"

"Well," I mumbled, still secretive back then about my own poetizing, "he's a poet."

"A poet," Herbie repeated. I nodded again, even more guiltily.

"Yeah," George snarled, "he *looked* like a fuckin' poet!"

Since I myself find it salutary now and then to "de-privilege"—de-authorize?—the overauthoritative author, it seems good enough to go on living among Herbies and Georges. Any time I catch some writer-fool prating of his or her "sensitivity" or "spontaneity" or "quest for deeper meanings," and more importantly, any time I find myself tempted to do the same, I turn not to the theorists' cloister but to that scene on George's lot. I think: Yes. A poet ought to *do* something. A poet ought to know the animals and the trees of the place—and to meet the people. And if he doesn't, he ought to be trying to.

Yet I must govern my sanctimony, having been so frustrated in my effort to meet the affable Hungarians, at least on their own linguistic ground.

4/15

I keep coming back to that matter of *ground*—linguistic, earthly, both at once. I spoke to a student today about a Robert Frost poem that's always had a hold on me. She admired it, but I couldn't help feeling she didn't "get" it, undeniably bright as she is. How could she, being urban, being Hungarian? So I wonder. And then I go on wondering: where does this leave me in the whole debate about shareable words?

Hyla Brook

By June our brook's run out of song and speed.
Sought for much after that, it will be found

Either to have gone groping underground
(And taken with it all the Hyla breed
That shouted in the mist a month ago,
Like ghost of sleigh bells in a ghost of snow)—
Or flourished and come up in jewelweed,
Weak foliage that is blown upon and bent,
Even against the way its waters went.
Its bed is left a faded paper sheet
Of dead leaves stuck together by the heat—
A brook to none but who remember long.
This as it will be seen is other far
Than with brooks taken otherwhere in song.
We love the things we love for what they are.

Brooks taken otherwhere in song may swell into the mighty poetic rivers of mighty poets—Spenser's Thames, Milton's Nile, Shelley's Arve, even Eliot's Mississippi, the strong brown god. The works in which they figure may flow on forever, avoiding the diminishment of the faded paper sheet. Be all that as it may, Frost loves his own brook for what it is.

I love it too, because I know the one, or one just like it. And I love it not only for whatever symbolism our New England genius may float upon it but also for its straightforward New England *brookiness,* from which—like Earl Bonness's figure of the tracks— it derives its primary power to move me, even as metaphor.

4/17

Today, I think, the hell with it! I'm not going to land on *any* sure ground, at least not theoretical ground. I keep getting lost.

But there's a freshet.

For forgotten reasons, my second son and I named it Bastard Brook, this skinny springtime rill. Far though it be from any trail, I can get to it and back in my sleep. Just now, if the nights have been mild, it sings Frost's sleighbell song—which I will remember long, and have, and do now, staring out on these streets, Budapest's spring ahead of our own, my window open, inscruta-

ble syllables drifting up from the sidewalks. Their speakers on this
fine day sound happy, happy in what *they* know.

I'd like to hike along Bastard this morning, attended or alone,
whether or not its minuscule waters are still locked in ice. I'd go as
far as the double-trunked rock maple on the south bank, and
maybe even farther, up and over height-of-land to Boulder City,
or right on east to Rattaway. If I did that, I'd travel ground from
which my own syllables could leap aloft, still however wearing, at
least metaphorically, the boots that had taken me, and them, so
high. Boots clotted with earth. And winter leaf. And late gray
snow.

4/22

> To the deconstructive critic, *presence* can mean *absence,* or anything
> else; *up* can mean *down,* or anything else; *mother* can mean *father,*
> or anything else. There is, the claim goes, "free play of signifiers,"
> which means that the critic can interpret without limit or con-
> straint and the author can never be in control of his language.

So writes Mark Turner.* And I think: Poor author. But even more
I think: Poor critic—for whom nothing can present itself with
sufficient definition or duration to be named, and thus to evoke
any pathos. However, Turner (God bless his good sense) may
bring my bereft theorist some cheer, by proving his or her responses to words to have "no serious basis in contemporary
linguistics or cognitive science." Neither of which, of course, I
have the slightest grasp on myself. But I can grasp what follows:

> Semantics is constrained by our models of ourselves and our
> worlds. We have models of *up* and *down* that are based on the ways
> our bodies actually function. Once the word "up" is given its

* In *Death is the Mother of Beauty* (University of Chicago Press, 1987), a *smart*
academic's book, which I idly picked off the shelf of my Hungarian office mate, a
linguist, and from which—on rereading my next few entries—I see I've all but
plagiarized.

meaning relative to our experience with gravity, it is not free to "slip" into its opposite.

Good. Now as I was saying, I'd like to head up the mountain, alongside my brook, slipping back down when *I* chose.

4/24

The strength of our words still resides in their truth to our most honest observations. "We love the things we love for what they are." And when it comes to metaphor, we can liken one thing to another, as Turner says, on the basis of family resemblance: there exists, for example, a transcultural reason that necessity should be the mother of invention and not its father.

If I have worried that few will recognize the family resemblance between a poem, say, and a hunt for gun-shy grouse, on home ground I can *find* those few. Not that we talk about poetry, but that we talk about the stuff of which poems are made. Mine anyhow.

4/29

Last fall, I started a new pointer bitch whose promise seems almost alarming. I hunted her most of the season on my own, and then finally met up with my old friend Landy Bartlett to show her off. By now the food was scarce in the covers, the game too, and as I watched my dog, I saw less the work she was doing— headstrong and blundery enough at moments—than the work that in time she *would* do, all somehow foretold in her manner.

The clocks gone back to standard, we'd lost our fall afternoons, and at 3:30 or so I had to pick my dog up. Landy and I sat for a spell on the tailgate, staring at the clean dark that walked at a human pace up the mountains, feeling a flake or two of snow on our wrists and faces, noting a heron who came languidly flapping out of a back pond, roost-bound early.

Signifiers.

"Well?" I asked at last, nodding toward my dog, still trembling and eager in her crate. "She going to be worth a nickel?"

Landy shook his head slowly for a few seconds, then he said exactly the right thing: "She just seems to float over the ground."

He meant home ground; or so I say here. Ground from which even cliché can float into eloquence, especially when traded among friends who have seen and loved the same things, who've made a lot of tracks together. On home ground, I know that in time I'll be able to frame even my solitary thoughts for such friends. As I guess I've been getting ready to do in this way-off place.

❦

It is the love of language that tugs me—and the language of love, even when expressed by companionable silence. These resemble another tug: I have hunted so long with them that I *must* have Joey on the right, Terry on the left. It's where they've always been. If the arrangement is upset, I feel my very body being moved by an invisible force, and I know—they've told me—they can feel that force too.

I handle the dogs, and so hold the center. More than once, I've thanked my own God for the miracle that I should be at the center of *anything,* should be able to speak, however briefly, from there.

5/1

Mayday, yet in mind the two men are snowshod. They disappear down the ghost of a drag road in Tough End. Earl is stoop-backed from his years of steadying a canoe or a free log in the boom. Creston is bearlike, barrel-chested, swaggery—no bottom, thin legs, big swinging arms. From my distance I can just make out the high murmur of his voice. And although the specific words are lost, I know the subject matter. I've walked that road myself.

With him. With Earl. With a few others.

Small thunder cuts my autumn doze on the porch.
Trotting by, two thoroughbreds—skittish, slender.
Dream is at once a heavy and delicate thing.

Donald's wrinkles could hold a week of rain.
Every fall, he told me, he'd bleed his horse.
A horse's waters thicken, summering over.

Or did he say he bled her after winter?
He spoke so much, so often, I ought to remember.
He said and said and said—I wasn't there.

A horse don't mind, she didn't mind, he said.
He'd make a jutting movement into air.
You put the knife-point, quick as you could, inside.

A Belgian would barely flinch, God was his witness.
He swore the roan mare didn't care.
Only a little prick in the palate's softness.

It's America, it's 1993.
Shy, the thoroughbred pair, and thin in the leg.
Softly, brightly clothed, the riders—like me.

Queenie, he whispered, she lowered her trunk of a neck.
Her look was almost bored, she seemed to yawn.
There stood a barrel, and blood came pouring down.

You needed to stanch it with alum right on time.
A horse was a thing you wanted not to lose.
By God you wanted a rugged horse back then.

Back then the trees got bigger than they do.
My road was just a path in the swamp, of course.
I wasn't there, repeat, not there, repeat.

You can't remember somebody now by a horse.
Not by a horse that really works, at least.
All I recall is Donald telling me of it.

Queenie, he'd whisper, repeating himself, he loved it.
You can't recall a person by a canoe.
I'm thinking now of George as well, awake.

Not a canoe you use, you really use.
You had to portage then from here to the lake.
Riverman, trapper, river of words, Bard.

The only roads were tote roads, so he said,
Repeating himself, repeating, I wasn't there.
You could borrow the loan of a horse if you were tired.

A timber horse, well-bled and -fed, was strong.
A Belgian would hardly pay a canoe attention.
You lashed it onto a sledge and drove it on.

George and Donald were there, who now are gone.
And this may be the realm of imagination.
When the Blackducks flew from the lake they covered the sun.

When a he-bear coughed in the woods, the great flanks trembled.
You threw wet trout on the garden to feed your corn.
You bled a horse in autumn, or was it spring?

Even in January the flanks would steam.
Good smell of flesh and blood, the hay, the hovel.
Vaporous song for New England. Imagination.

Useless, swift and helpless, the thoroughbreds.
Dream's domain: song and talk; museum.
You have to make sure that too much blood don't spill.

They told me so, they laughed, they frowned, they said.
There were rocks, rapids, currents you couldn't feel.
Solid things and spectral, redundant winds.

There were widow-makers, limbs that fell without sound.
Sometimes, though, the horses seemed to hear.
Sometimes they'd bolt, and a ton of horse can maim.

That much horse is a delicate thing all the same.
So Donald always suggested, I wasn't there.
You could fix any boat you didn't completely lose.

Sometimes I lose it, even the shadow from slumber.
Canvas and cedar, ash ribs, gunwales of spruce.
Mist, recalls—Donald and George, New England.

Horses, canoes, talk, men, museum.
Thunder, wood-scrap, green cloth going under.
The old men's regal faces could hold the rain.

He twitches the horse's lip, the knife jabs in.
Riders wave to me from the road all cheerful.
I think the Belgian mare's big legs will buckle.

I think we're late, and blood brims over the barrel.
Its stain is the shade of these Indian Summer maples.
It's 1993, the canoe is fragile.

The spindly trot comes liquid through autumn air.
Words I repeat and repeat for George and Donald.
I say and say. And say who wasn't there.

HONESTY

An Afterword

WHAT IS THE LAST BOOK you read? Which movie did you see most recently? Who's your favorite singer? I can't confidently reproduce the full list of our banal questions, much less what I wrote in response. And while I remember the two we intended more seriously—what big change will happen in your life by the time you dig this up? what single wish would you make right now?—I recall my answer to the latter alone: *Happiness for my children.*

We buried the time capsule in 1982, during a short campout at Third Lake. My son, ten years old then, slept under a tent on the sandbeach with his pal Johnny; my fiancée and I and my daughter Erika, five, slept in a cabin that had once belonged to dear Creston MacArthur, for whom the son was named.

Though now, the decade flown and more, Erika writes like an angel herself, that August she was still mystified by the written word. She needed help, and she got it from the woman who'd soon be her stepmother. I recall how annoying she found such dependence; hers would be the only answers known to another person. Yet the little girl's unhappiness seemed nothing beside her brother's rage and pain, his far more embittering mystification. How in God's name, after all, could his flesh-and-blood father mean to marry a different woman from his flesh-and-blood mother?

Yet it was not only for domestic reasons that I found our stay

hard. Some of the best moments of my younger life had transpired on this very spot—and had come to a heartbreaking halt
with Creston MacArthur's death in 1976. Six short years, but such
a lot of water over the dam! Even today the platitude seems right
as I think of Third Lake, the rivermen driving their booms out of
it and down the Machias.

A son of summer folks, of course, I never saw the drive—except
inwardly, through the visions that Creston and others planted in
my mind. Pickpoles. Rough women waiting at the bridges. Some
bareknuckle flareup over a stolen whetstone. Cream of Tartar
biscuits and beans four times each day. Arthur, the Passamaquoddy
who always set the dynamite charge to break a jam, who "trotted
them logs like a mink would," as one old river hand put it.

When I first heard such particulars, they struck me with an
almost frightening vividness; I needed actual force of will to
remember I'd not made that run myself, and even now—less
susceptible to such delusion—I remain stirred by the scenes I
once imagined, and will forever.

The oldtimers let a big head build, then opened the gates,
everything racing seaward in a mass.

§

There's a small marsh—or heath, as the Scots-derived natives
say—not far upshore from the Third Lake cabin. Creston and I
watched that wetland in many a summer's dusk, just to see what
would walk into it, or fly: cow moose liked the place, despite its
mosquitoes and gadflies, though for some reason no grown bull
ever showed there; it was a favorite too of mergansers, who'd
scrabble after the plentiful frogs, churning dark mud till we
smelled it even from our distance; deer drank from the red water
pooled on the heath's inland edge, just under boughs of crowding
cedar.

But things were different in the summer of the owl. He would
drop from a hemlock behind the cabin, drifting in his absolute,
uncanny silence over our heads, cruising the cattails and grasses of
the marsh, low as a harrier, at last flinging up a wing and banking
sharply earthward and taking flight again—all one motion—with
an indistinguishable small something in his grip.

Inside that deep plumage, the great horned owl is actually dove-sized. Deadly though he be, then, he'll not take on a big duck. And yet the August I speak of was a month of no mergansers. Even the moose and deer stayed absent. We'd see nothing but dusk's fierce raptor, who worried the amphibians and rodents to literal death, for he never rose from that slue empty-clawed.

"Find me a man that hunts like that," Creston mused one evening, "and I'll stove his gun for him."

I could not see the man's big grin, backlit as he was by the last of sunlight, but I remember somehow *feeling* it like the sudden breeze that kicked up, bending the marshweeds our way, ferrying the smell to us of the heath, a rankness I still inhale like perfume: smell of a bird dog after a hardworking day, of a duck blind at dawn, of a mudbar where the river slowly eddies and big trout sip from the backwash, challenging a cast's precision. It speaks of a world ever shrinking, the one not yet locked under asphalt.

Once the owl's lethal patrol was finished, I remember how abruptly the sun tumbled, the way it does in a place with lots of sky and a ridgey horizon. If we'd worn any, we could have set our watches by the bird, whose rite was constant night after night, or at least seemed so whenever we came into camp—as it turned out we'd never do again, not in each other's company.

❧

Since the summer of our owl, I have returned three times to the Third Lake camp.

In October of '76, eight months after Creston's death, I went out alone, meaning to do some jumpshooting in Mutton Cove and Dead Stream and along the shallow north shore of the Middleground, the same spots in which we'd so often scouted ducks together. But there seemed omens everywhere, and they distracted me, above all and unaccountably an old-fashioned hightop Ked sneaker, its lace strung to Creston's clothesline. I remember wondering what on earth he could have used *that* for, and when. It wasn't simple bafflement, though, that kept me sleepless. Sometime during the small hours, I watched a squall rush from the Machias dam across to the campyard, and in its unseasonable flashes of lightning I beheld the wind-driven shoe, wheeling in ragged orbit, the sight of it flooding me with unnameable fear, and a sadness weighty as iron.

I had three days to spare, and come dawn I found ducks enough as ordinarily to keep me interested for the full of that time. Yet I paddled out before noontime, shivering in a rain that had turned to quiet, frigid drizzle. In the bow my retriever shivered too, his face so dark and mournful I dreamed he knew my grief.

$$\mathscr{X}$$

The Ked still hung there on my next trip, in that August of '82 when we hid our capsule. Though by now it had a different aspect, the winters having changed it from black to ghostly, it continued oddly to oppress me, and during the first afternoon— while the rest were swimming—I walked to the clothesline, open jackknife in hand. And yet somehow I couldn't cut that icon down.

On the following day we turned to our questionnaire. When we had finished, we put our papers in a sealable plastic bag. Next we stuck that bag in a small coffee can, which we wrapped in yet a bigger plastic bag. Then we deposited the smaller can in a larger, and finally swaddled the whole works in a big green leaf sack.

We decided to make our hole just west of Creston's cabin, where the sandbeach comes to a point. A great pyramid stone stands there, well above high water line, so that the rock marked a good, dry site. The digging was easy, fun: even Erika took a hand in it.

$$\mathscr{X}$$

My third visit came in 1992, ten years later. Though the decade passed with dizzying speed, Georgia Pacific managed in that short span to carve more roads in the back country than one would have thought feasible. One of these ran to the Third Lake shore not far from where our capsule lay buried. I drove it, muttering the whole way, passing the murderous chipping operations, the clearcuts with their trompe l'oeil facades of reseeded growth on the shoulders. To approach that water by car and not canoe didn't feel right in the first place. It was shameful of me to accede to the convenience of a road—the kind of convenience that's ruining wildness all over the world.

Yet what canoe would hold us all now? My son Creston, six feet six inches tall, was spending the summer doing research for his favorite college professor. His friend Johnny, a U.S. Marine now, was off in some barracks. But my daughter Erika was with us again, along with the three small siblings who'd been born since '82, one of them a six-month-old baby girl with her father's androgynous name. We'd brought my twin twelve-year-old nieces for good measure, making an outing of it—some swimming, exploring, food. After all, only Erika and Robin and I had been present at the capsule's interment, and of these I'd been the single one to have known Creston MacArthur as more than a name.

We finally fetched up at lakeside. A gigantic A-frame, surrounded by all-terrain vehicles, stood there, strange as cancer. I knocked on the door, but no one responded. Stepping over to the bluff, I looked down on a row of aluminum motorboats. A plastic soda bottle and two Bud empties rolled back and forth in the rote; but no one was down there either.

When I went back to the car, our gang spilled out. I pointed west along the shore. "Just walk that way a few hundred yards," I said. The kids took off like hounds, all but little Sydney, whom I loaded into a carrying pack.

Grabbing the spade, I stood in my tracks for a moment, facing away from my car, from the new building, from the ranks of three-wheelers and powerboats. I could make out the owl's marsh in the near distance; somebody had driven a post in its middle and strung a cable from there up to the knoll where I stood. I guessed the rig was for one of those running deer effigies: you let the thing slide on its wire and then shoot. You aim behind the metal foreshoulder at the sham heart.

The baby fell quickly asleep on my back. Strolling downhill to where the high tier flattens and joins the beach, I stopped again, wanting to give the others a generous headstart, wanting to walk that edge alone, slow and speechless. Or maybe not to walk it at all.

On my desk at home I have a photograph of Creston, his canoe nosed ashore just at that spot. Wearing a green-plaid mackinaw and a hueless baseball cap, he sits in the stern. His hands are raised, and he sights along an imaginary shotgun. The picture catches him in the midst of one of his countless hunting tales—I can't remember which, and it doesn't matter: it fills me with joy and melancholy anyhow.

Crosslake, I noticed a soaring bird. An eagle, I imagined, but when I squinted it turned into a gull, its squawks borne my way by the south wind. That blow bore weather too. The day, which had started bright, was graying fast, and the change made me think of another time many years gone, over there on the Middleground.

I'd come out with Creston's uncle George MacArthur. I called him uncle too. Each of us, unbeknownst to the other, had brought a fifth of whiskey, and we lay on the beach till midnight, trading talk and song, drinking his jug down to empty. And then, fools that we were, we drank down mine. We lolled there till dawn, which broke into south wind like this. And then came the piddling rain.

A boy, I could handle such hours of carousing, though they'd maybe kill me today. George was in his seventies, and on the trip home he swore they damn near did kill him. I can still see him in the bow of our boat, a short but huge-shouldered man, his whole frame slouching. Every fifth stroke or so he points his paddle toward the sky, letting lakewater run down the shaft and into his parched mouth.

And yet forever after George would claim that that misery had been worth it—for the time we had on our trip, for the things we sang and said, which I'll bet were among the best ever to pass between us. The words have flown from memory; indeed, most of them were likely gone by morning; but the conversation counted much less in any case than the fact that we held it where names of land- and watermarks provided all the eloquence anyone could need: Freeze-to-Death Island. The Burn, Washington Bald Mountain, Slaughter Point. Who cared about our talk's specific content?

Yet even back then was I not a man for content? I believed a writer's job was to take the impressions of a time and setting and to recall or invent their specifics, to give them back the voices that had fallen mute or that never existed in the first place.

Today I smile ruefully at certain of my old naivetés. I quickly learned, for example, that there's no such thing as the voice of nature or even of place—or none at least that will yield to human translation. And yet there did remain the voices of *people* whose lives were drenched in the natural. Years ago, maybe during the course of that very liquory night with George, I surmised that I might render the rhythms and cadences of those voices without having to imitate them exactly. That it would in any case be worth finding out.

❦

Hearing a faint flat vowel over the breeze, I reeled my mind back to now, to 1992: down the lakeshore, I could see small figures waving towels and bits of clothing; what I'd heard was likely the *a* in "Dad," the children calling to me, who held the shovel. How long must I have been stuck in my reverie, oblivious even of the baby on my back?

To travel toward the point was another act of will, for I couldn't cover ten yards of beach without coming on something to stop me again in my tracks. Will, however, prevailed.

Until I came in sight of the campyard.

Just over there lay the rocks Creston and I used to sit on as we scanned our marsh. Our moose. Our deer. Our sheldrakes gigging blackback frogs. Our owl, so lethal, quiet, punctual. There too stood the outdoor fireplace, where we broiled two duck one October evening. Oh, we cooked plenty of others over such a blaze, but that pair proved somehow the best of the many, probably because we ate them just after the finest duck-hunting day of my life.

Uphill, tucked just under the hemlock canopy, was the cabin itself, timbers fitted on the vertical: when a man builds a camp all alone he can't handle a long log on the horizontal; he makes a sill, then balances an end of his stick on it with one hand and hammers with the other—a tricky, tentative business. Everything can fall down on you before you know it.

The lowness of the doorway; the faded verdigris oakum chinking the walls; the beachstone chimney; the sagging wharf from which loud children were jumping now into water; the rotted outdoor table; an axe still lying on the porch, its handle fretted by porcupines who craved the dead man's traces of sweat.

Physical particulars damn near undid me. I huffed suddenly, uncontrollably, exactly as I have done each time I've seen a child burst out of the womb.

"What's the matter?" It was Erika.

"Oh, a lot of memories," I whispered, forcing a self-dismissive grin.

My wife kissed me on the cheek and rubbed my shoulders. Her imagination has always equaled my own, at least.

For all the moment's pathos, Robin's kindness reminded me that I was a lucky man, and had always been, in so many ways. By this very lake, for example, I'd once decided to be a writer; and now something was all but writing itself as I stood again on its shore. There weren't many, I guessed, who could walk just so into a waiting metaphorical scheme: the past unburying itself.

※

That scheme, however, was soon skewed. I dug so wide and so deep around our rock that at last I feared it might fall in upon me. But I could not find our time capsule.

At length I flung myself on the sand, exhausted not so much from physical effort as self-contempt. How like me, this fiasco! How often had I discovered a new bird cover, for example, and then—all eagerness to hunt it—subsequently forgotten the roads I'd taken to get there? How many days had I spent in searches, sometimes vain, to rediscover places? How often had I vowed to notice the world more carefully?

Yet here I was, so sure I knew the paths I'd followed—so profoundly wrong again. And if one memory could fail me like this, what faith might I put in other memories? Perhaps the past could never *be* exhumed. That was a dispiriting thought for an elegist, enough so that I imagined laying all the pages I'd ever written end to end along this beach. They'd reach a considerable distance, well past the owl's heath. If I waited till the wind swung west again, I could touch a match to the first sheet, then watch the flame run back, against the way I'd come.

Except in my very occasional forays into fiction, I have always felt an obligation to factual truth in my writing, to honesty in that sense. There is nothing moralistic in such a feeling; it is only that I find it enabling. Standing on that particular lakeshore, before my dead friend's camp, I felt that enablement buckle.

Earlier in the afternoon, for instance, I'd remembered a certain day of duck-hunting as the finest in my life, but in what, I now wondered, did its fineness consist? The two birds we broiled over the old fireplace may have tasted as wonderful as they did primarily because they were the only spoils from a miserably uncomfortable trip: I learned among other things why Freeze-to-Death Island had gotten its name, stationed there while Creston jumped a black-duck raft in Mutton cove, all the birds spooking before he could get within range, and none flying over that cold clump of rocks where I huddled. Then I tried my unsuccessful hand at sneaking on a flock, this one rafted in the Eastern Arm, while Creston hid in the high-bush blueberries on the bank of Dead Stream. He never fired a shot.

Toward dusk we crippled a whistler, but though my Labrador searched for a long, long time, it got away, went off somewhere to die in pain, alone.

I remembered that just before bedtime we drank a toddy—bourbon, hot water, and sugar. How good, how warming it seemed. And how badly I wanted more, wanted, say, the two full bottles that Uncle George and I had consumed that night on the Middleground. Since I was onto issues of honesty, it seemed worth recalling that that trip might well have marked an early chapter in the dazing subsequent years of my battle with booze.

And booze, having done well to break up my first marriage, in some measure engendered the feelings my firstborn had tried and failed to contain when we buried that time capsule in 1982: pain, anger, pure mystification. Supposing we *had* found the buried writings: what might they have said about the past, and how much pleasure might I take in it? I didn't need to tax myself much to imagine the sort of thing that that firstborn boy had recorded as his biggest wish: for my fiancée to crawl into Third Lake and become a white perch, a turtle, a polliwog—anything but what she was.

My own big wish, for my children to be happy, extended perhaps above all to that son Creston, for I knew how far out of reach such a prospect seemed in 1982. However brilliantly he now fares, back then it must have seemed as though someone had died, a death as tragic to him as that other Creston's to me.

Lying next to that large gap in the sand, yet another line from Emily Dickinson occurred to me: "Tell all the truth, but tell it slant." Maybe, I thought, that's what I've been doing for a long time. It was a hopeful notion, according to which my bittersweet recalls of a George or Creston MacArthur, those voices murmuring in the unspecific half-light, might be truth purged of its nagging contradictions.

And yet the more sobering possibility remained that I could mention nothing with certainty beyond the names of such men, the names of some other persons, and certain indelible facts, however plain: an owl; a cabin; a lake; an island or two; a basketball shoe wheeling crazily on its lace. I could be honest at least about the likes of these, and to such likes must I even now repair—again and again—as I dig up the past, or try.

the gauzy lichen here
to mask this granite
I know I will not save
invading
as often will be hare's
and cat's
thin trail out
that I may leave
than they incise
in easy passing
nor greater wound
in any less than
today I will not prey
my way may do
but let it do at least

took years
patient earth
nor cure
yet today my path
and deer's
described by scat and track
thin trail back
no greater scar
on scarp and peak
unpursued
than weather makes
fevered mood
nor storm
no earthly good
no harm

UNIVERSITY PRESS OF NEW ENGLAND publishes books under its own imprint and is the publisher for Brandeis University Press, Brown University Press, University of Connecticut, Dartmouth College, Middlebury College Press, University of New Hampshire, University of Rhode Island, Tufts University, University of Vermont, Wesleyan University Press, and Salzburg Seminar.

Library of Congress Cataloging-in-Publication Data

Lea, Sydney.
    Hunting the whole way home : notes from a life outside / Sydney Lea.
        p.   cm.
    ISBN 0-87451-689-7
    1. Hunting.   2. Outdoor life.   I. Title.
SK33.L38   1994
799.2—dc20   94-20491
♾

Photo by Bruce Paul Richards

About the Author

Sydney Lea is the author of five books of poetry, most recently
The Blainville Testament (1992) and *Prayer for the Little City*
(1991), and of the novel *A Place in Mind* (1989). Recipient of
awards from the Guggenheim, Rockefeller, and Fulbright foundations, Lea was founder and for thirteen years editor of *New
England Review.* Though he has taught at Dartmouth, Yale, and
Middlebury, he claims to have done some of his most rewarding
research among the woods and waters of Vermont, New Hampshire, and Maine, where he has hunted, fished, run sporting dogs,
and guided all his adult life.